Smartphone Users Immersed In Video Apps

Smartphone Users Immersed In Video Apps

Rafeal Mechlore

Grace Publishers

CONTENTS

INDEX

8.1 How advancements in technology continue to shape video app usage.
8.2 Emerging trends and future possibilities.

Chapter 9: Society's Adaptation to Change
9.1 The societal and cultural implications of smartphone immersion.
9.2 How society is responding to these transformations.

Introduction

The cell phone, a development that has re-imagined present day life, has turned into a basic piece of our day to day presence. In the range of years and years, it has changed from a straightforward specialized gadget into a multifunctional computerized buddy, consistently coordinating into each feature of our lives. Among the heap of capacities cell phones offer, video applications have arisen as a predominant power, changing the manner in which we consume and cooperate with media. In this steadily developing computerized scene, the combination of cell phone innovation and video applications has led to a social shift, rethinking how we experience diversion, training, social collaboration, and data dispersal. This change has impacted individual clients as well as sent swells through businesses, molding the substance we consume, the advertising techniques utilized, and the cultural standards that administer our communications.

The excursion that carried us to this point is set apart by quick progressions in portable innovation and the multiplication of fast web availability. The underlying motivation behind a cell phone, which was basically voice correspondence, has given way to another period where cell phones are courses to a tremendous computerized universe. In the mid 2000s, the idea of watching recordings on a cell phone was a far off dream, compelled by restricted handling power, capacity limit, and information speeds. Nonetheless, with every emphasis of cell phone innovation, the possibility to transfer, record, and alter recordings extended, bringing the film and TV experience straightforwardly into the centers of clients' hands.

The development of video applications on cell phones addresses a change in outlook by they way we consume content. These applications, which incorporate online entertainment stages, real time features, instructive devices, and media sources, have re-imagined our relationship with screens, as we create some distance from customary TVs and embrace the versatility, personalization, and intuitiveness presented by our cell phones. In this advanced age, the cell phone screen has turned into our window to the world, and the video application is the entry through which we peer into it.

One of the vital main impetuses behind the rising submersion in video applications is the sheer comfort they offer. Cell phone clients can now convey whole libraries of movies, Network programs, and recordings in their pockets, open whenever, in any spot. The accommodation of on-request video real time features has changed our survey propensities, permitting us to watch what we need, when we need it. Marathon watching has turned into a social peculiarity, as clients jump into whole times of their number one series with a couple of taps on their screens. This change in perspective has disturbed the conventional transmission model as well as prompted the formation of altogether new types of content and narrating, as producers and content makers adjust to the changing utilization examples of their crowd.

Moreover, the personalization and suggestion calculations utilized by video applications have additionally upgraded our inundation. These calculations bridle the force of large information and AI to arrange content in light of our inclinations, seeing history, and segment data. In doing as such, they assist clients with finding new happy as well as make closed quarters where people are presented to data that lines up with their current convictions and interests. This personalization can have both positive and pessimistic results, as it can improve our client experience by acquainting us with content we probably won't have in any case experienced, yet it can likewise prompt data air pockets and channel bubbles that build up our current predispositions and limit openness to different viewpoints.

The submersion in video applications reaches out past diversion to envelop training. With the coming of huge open internet based courses (MOOCs) and e-learning stages, cell phone clients can get to an abundance of instructive substance readily available. These stages offer courses, talks, and instructional exercises on a large number of subjects, empowering deep rooted mastering and abilities improvement. The adaptability and openness of cell phone based schooling have democratized picking up, making it feasible for people all over the planet to obtain information and abilities that were once restricted to conventional instructive establishments.

In addition, the intelligence and commitment of video applications have changed how we connect with instructive substance. Gamification, intelligent tests, and conversation discussions inside these applications make learning more captivating as well as take into account evaluation and input, improving the general opportunity for growth. Subsequently, the cell phone has turned into an incredible asset for both conventional schooling and independent learning, with the possibility to connect instructive holes and enable people to seek after their scholarly and proficient desires.

While video applications offer accommodation and personalization, they additionally bring up significant issues about how they shape our social associations. The universality of cell phones and virtual entertainment stages has changed the manner in which we convey and associate with others. Video calls, live web based, and stories have become fundamental parts of our advanced connections, empowering us to see and be found progressively. Video applications give a stage to sharing individual encounters, feelings, and imaginative articulations, encouraging a feeling of having a place and network that rises above geological limits. In any case, the steady openness to arranged and glorified portrayals of others' lives via virtual entertainment can likewise prompt social examination and insecurities, affecting psychological wellness.

The ascent of video applications has likewise re-imagined the idea of "powerhouses" and superstars. People who gain unmistakable quality through stages like YouTube, Instagram, and TikTok can gather enormous followings and apply huge impact over their crowd. These computerized characters frequently obscure the lines among validness and execution, introducing painstakingly created personas that can be adapted through brand organizations and supports. The power and reach of these forces to be reckoned with have upset conventional publicizing models, as brands perceive the worth of powerhouse advertising in associating with more youthful and all the more carefully sagacious crowds. This, thusly, has led to conversations about straightforwardness, validness, and the obligations of forces to be reckoned with in forming public discernments and ways of behaving.

The universality of video applications additionally presents huge difficulties and valuable open doors for news and reporting. While these applications give a stage to fast news dispersal and resident reporting, they have likewise led to worries about the spread of falsehood, counterfeit news, and channel bubbles. The speed at which data goes through video applications can enhance the effect of tales and misleading accounts, making it progressively hard to perceive reality from fiction. In this time of computerized data, media education has turned into a basic expertise, as clients should explore a scene where news and diversion frequently join, testing conventional thoughts of objectivity and editorial honesty.

The vivid idea of video applications has likewise influenced the promoting business. As customary promotion designs, like TV ads and print ads, have become less successful in catching shoppers' consideration, publicists have gone to video applications for of arriving at their main interest groups. In-stream advertisements, supported content, and powerhouse joint efforts have become normal procedures for brands to draw in with purchasers. Moreover, information investigation and focusing on instruments permit publicists to fit their messages to explicit socioeconomics, further obscuring the lines among content and publicizing. This has raised worries about client protection, information security, and the moral ramifications of information driven publicizing rehearses.

The connection between video applications and psychological well-being is a subject of developing concern. The consistent openness to screens, the habit-forming nature of web-based entertainment looking over, and the tensions related with online self-show can prompt issues like computerized dependence, nervousness, and sorrow. These worries have incited conversations about computerized detox, care, and mindful screen using time effectively, as people endeavor to track down a harmony between their computerized and disconnected lives.

Past individual clients, the drenching in video applications has more extensive cultural ramifications. It has changed how we draw in with legislative issues, as virtual entertainment stages and live-streaming have become apparatuses for political prepa-ration, activism, and mindfulness. The fast scattering of recordings portraying social and political occasions significantly affects public talk, impacting the manner in which we see and answer issues like civil rights, basic liberties, and ecological worries.

Additionally, the impact of video applications has molded the scene of the diversion and content creation enterprises. Conventional media organizations, when the guards of amusement, are currently rivaling advanced local stages for crowd consideration. The ascent of client produced content has engaged people to become content makers, testing the customary progressive system of media creation. This democratization of content creation has prompted the development of different voices and stories, yet it has likewise raised worries about copyright encroachment, licensed innovation, and the maintainability of inventive vocations.

Chapter 1

The Digital Era's Transformation

The computerized time, portrayed by the fast and unavoidable reconciliation of computerized advances into all parts of human existence, has introduced a significant change that contacts basically every feature of our reality. In this period, our reality is characterized by the tenacious walk of advancement, the ubiquity of interconnected gadgets, and the unlimited open doors made conceivable by the computerized unrest. As we explore this steadily developing scene, it is essential to comprehend the significant changes it has fashioned, and the manners by which it has reshaped our general public, economy, culture, and individual lives.

At the core of the computerized period's change is the digitization of data and the extraordinary access we now need to it. The digitization interaction has seen everything from text and pictures to music and video changed over into a computerized design, considering capacity, transmission, and control at a scale and speed beforehand impossible. In this computerized world, information rules, and the capacity to gather, process, and use it has turned into a strong wellspring of force and impact. This change has modified our relationship with data, making it both an important asset and an expected wellspring of weakness, as issues of information protection, security, and possession become the overwhelming focus.

Also, the computerized time has reshaped the manner in which we impart and cooperate with each other. The ascent of the web and the multiplication of virtual entertainment stages have democratized correspondence, empowering people and gatherings to associate across huge distances, share thoughts, and participate in worldwide discussions. These computerized stages have likewise worked with the making of virtual networks, where people with shared interests can shape bonds and trade data, encouraging a feeling of having a place that rises above geographic limits.

All the while, the computerized period has changed the manner in which we consume and create content. The coming of web based distributing, contributing to a blog, and online entertainment has permitted anybody with a web association with be a substance maker, leading to a different exhibit of voices and stories. This change has upset conventional media ventures and tested their gatekeeping job, taking into consideration more prominent democratization of data spread and diversion. In any case, it has additionally prompted worries about the believability of content, the spread of falsehood, and the manageability of imaginative vocations in a period set apart by computerized robbery and content immersion.

Financially, the advanced period has prodded tremendous development and the production of new ventures. The innovation area has arisen as a force to be reckoned with, with organizations like Apple, Amazon, Google, Facebook, and others molding the worldwide economy and using enormous impact. The appearance of web based business has reformed the manner in which we shop, with online commercial centers and advanced installment frameworks making it conceivable to trade labor and products with unrivaled accommodation. The gig economy has likewise flourished, offering new types of work and pay age, however it has raised worries about employer stability, work freedoms, and the disintegration of conventional business models.

The advanced time's change of the economy reaches out to fund also. Advanced monetary forms, like Bitcoin and blockchain innovation, have arisen as potential disruptors of the customary banking and monetary frameworks. These advancements guarantee more prominent security, straightforwardness, and openness in monetary exchanges, while additionally introducing administrative difficulties and vulnerabilities. Decentralized finance (DeFi) has picked up speed, with the possibility to reshape how we save, contribute, and manage monetary exchanges.

In the domain of medical services, the computerized period has introduced another time of information driven medication. Electronic wellbeing records, telemedicine, wearable gadgets, and wellbeing applications can possibly work on quiet consideration, conclusion, and treatment. The assortment and examination of huge measures of wellbeing information can illuminate clinical exploration and upgrade how we might interpret infections and general wellbeing. In any case, this change is joined by worries about information protection, the security of wellbeing data, and the potential for segregation in light of wellbeing information.

The change of training in the advanced period has been downright progressive. Internet learning stages, enormous open web-based courses (MOOCs), and virtual homerooms have extended admittance to schooling, permitting people from varying backgrounds to obtain information and abilities. This change can possibly democratize training, separate topographical boundaries, and give deep rooted learning open doors. Nonetheless, it additionally presents difficulties connected with the computerized partition, evenhanded admittance to instructive assets, and the requirement for new educational ways to deal with draw in and support online students actually.

Moreover, the computerized time significantly affects the manner in which we work and team up. Remote work, empowered by advanced innovations, has become progressively common, changing our ideas of the work environment, work hours, and balance between serious and fun activities. The cooperation devices and cloud-based stages have made it feasible for groups to cooperate from various areas, and the gig economy has re-imagined the customary boss worker relationship. This change has suggestions for work freedoms, the requirement for advanced abilities, and the reconsideration of working environment standards and practices.

The advanced time's change stretches out to the domain of administration and governmental issues. The ascent of web-based entertainment stages and advanced apparatuses for political commitment has given voice to residents and enabled them to partake in political cycles. Be that as it may, it has likewise raised worries about the spread of deception, online provocation, and the effect of advanced protected, closed off environments on political polarization. The advanced time has carried new difficulties to issues of a majority rule government, network safety, and the requirement for administrative systems that can adjust to the speed of innovative change.

With regards to culture, the computerized period has changed the manner in which we make, consume, and share workmanship and amusement. The web has turned into a huge stage for inventive articulation, with specialists, performers, movie producers, and essayists sharing their work straightforwardly with worldwide crowds. Web-based features have disturbed customary models of content dissemination, presenting on-request admittance to an immense range of motion pictures, music, and network shows. This change has reshaped the media and media outlets, rethinking how we find and draw in with social substance. Nonetheless, it has additionally raised worries about the monetary manageability of imaginative callings and the requirement for new models of pay and copyright insurance.

The advanced time's change likewise has expansive ramifications for security and guard. Digital fighting, information breaks, and the potential for advanced assaults on basic framework have become squeezing worries for countries and associations. The dependence on computerized advances for guard and knowledge has both upgraded capacities and presented weaknesses, requiring another way to deal with public safety and worldwide relations in the computerized age.

The advanced time has introduced a period of remarkable information observation and security concerns. The huge measure of individual data gathered by innovation organizations and government offices has brought up issues about individual freedoms, assent, and the potential for misuse. The pressure between the craving for security and the assurance of common freedoms has led to banters about encryption, information maintenance, and the harmony among protection and reconnaissance in the advanced age.

In addition, the computerized period's change is firmly connected to the natural difficulties within recent memory. The multiplication of electronic gadgets, server farms, and the energy expected for computerized framework has huge ecological effects. The requirement for manageable practices in innovation, from energy-proficient server farms to dependable e-garbage removal, has become progressively dire as we stand up to the real factors of environmental change.

As we consider the computerized period's change, thinking about the moral and philosophical ramifications of these changes is fundamental. The advanced domain suggests significant conversation starters about character, credibility, and the idea of reality itself. As we draw in with virtual conditions, man-made brainpower, and expanded and computer generated reality, we are tested to reexamine our relationship with the actual world and the limits between the advanced and the genuine.

1.1 The evolution of smartphones and their impact on society.

The cell phone, a pocket-sized innovative wonder, has gone through a surprising development since its initiation, changing the manner in which we convey as well as the manner in which we live, work, and connect with the world. Brought into the world from the union of portable communication, figuring power, and creative plan, the cell phone has turned into a vital piece of current culture, reshaping how we explore our day to day routines. In this conversation, we will investigate the development of cell phones, from their initial beginnings to the present, and analyze the significant effect they have had on society.

The historical backdrop of cell phones can be followed back to the mid-twentieth century when the idea of a compact, remote specialized gadget started to come to fruition. While early cell phones were huge, weighty, and restricted to voice calls, they established the groundwork for what might ultimately turn into the cell phone. The excursion towards the advanced cell phone was set apart by a few key turns of events.

The main cell phone call was made by Martin Cooper, a Motorola leader, in 1973. Cooper's gadget, known as the Motorola DynaTAC 8000X, was enormous and unwieldy by the present principles, weighing almost two pounds and bragging a sticker price $3,995. It was a huge achievement in remote correspondence, yet it was a long way from what we currently consider a cell phone.

The change from cell phones to cell phones was continuous and driven by propels in innovation and buyer interest. During the 1990s, individual advanced aides (PDAs) like the Palm Pilot arose, joining fundamental registering capacities with versatile communication. These gadgets could store contacts, schedules, and notes, yet they coming up short on web availability and media includes that characterize current cell phones.

The genuine defining moment accompanied the presentation of the BlackBerry, which consolidated email usefulness with versatile communication. The BlackBerry, created by Exploration Moving (presently BlackBerry Restricted), was the principal gadget to procure the moniker "cell phone." It furnished clients with an actual console for message input and became inseparable from versatile email correspondence.

In 2007, Apple's iPhone arisen as a unique advantage. With its smooth plan, multi-contact screen, and the presentation of the Application Store, the iPhone re-imagined what a cell phone could be. It united communication and email as well as web perusing, media playback, and a wide exhibit of utilizations. The iPhone's prosperity ignited another period in cell phone advancement, with different organizations hurrying to contend and improve.

The years following the iPhone's delivery saw a blast in cell phone innovation. Highlights like high-goal cameras, GPS route, voice collaborators, and high level sensors became standard. Android, Google's versatile working framework, gave a powerful option in contrast to Apple's iOS, cultivating rivalry and broadening the cell phone market.

The idea of the "cell phone" developed past being simply a specialized gadget into a multifunctional instrument that has changed virtually every part of society. Here are a few key regions where cell phones have had a tremendous effect.

Correspondence and Social Connection: Cell phones have changed the manner in which we convey, empowering voice and message correspondence, as well as media informing through stages like WhatsApp, Facebook Courier, and Snapchat. Online entertainment applications have become vital to how we associate with companions, family, and the world. The consistent network worked with by cell phones has changed the idea of connections and social communications, taking into consideration constant updates and prompt reactions.

Data Access: Cell phones have turned into our essential door to the web. We can get to a huge storehouse of information, news, and data with only a couple of taps on our screens. The capacity to look for data in a hurry has changed the manner in which we learn, decide, and remain informed about the world.

Diversion: Cell phones have become compact amusement habitats, permitting us to stream films, Programs, and music, as well as mess around and read digital books. With top notch shows, strong processors, and vivid sound, cell phones have re-imagined how we engage ourselves. Web-based features like Netflix and Spotify have become easily recognized names, and portable gaming has developed into an extravagant industry.

Photography and Videography: The cell phone's underlying cameras have made it more straightforward than at any other time for individuals to report their lives. The nature of cell phone cameras has improved decisively, and numerous leader gadgets presently rival conventional cameras with regards to picture quality and elements. Cell phones have additionally democratized content creation, permitting clients to catch and impart minutes to the world.

Route and Area Administrations: GPS innovation coordinated into cell phones has changed the manner in which we explore and track down our direction. Planning applications like Google Guides have become fundamental for getting bearings, finding new spots, and in any event, observing traffic conditions progressively. Area based administrations have changed enterprises like ride-sharing and food conveyance.

Work and Efficiency: Cell phones have empowered another period of remote work and efficiency. Email, schedule, and assignment the executives applications have made it feasible for individuals to work from anyplace, obscuring the lines among work and individual life. Joint effort devices like Leeway and Zoom have re-imagined how groups impart and work together.

Wellbeing and Wellness: Wellbeing and wellness applications on cell phones have enabled people to screen their prosperity. Wearable gadgets that sync with cell phones can follow steps, pulse, rest examples, from there, the sky is the limit. These devices have added to a developing familiarity with individual wellbeing and wellness.

Web based business and Portable Installments: Cell phones have changed the manner in which we shop, from online retail to versatile installments. Online business monsters like Amazon and Alibaba have seen dangerous development, and versatile installment frameworks like Apple Pay and research Wallet have made it simple to make buys with a tap of the telephone.

Schooling: Cell phones have stretched out admittance to training through portable learning applications and online courses. Understudies, everything being equal, can get to instructive assets, take courses, and obtain new abilities utilizing their cell phones. This change can possibly span instructive holes and deal long lasting learning valuable open doors.

Supportability: While cell phones have added to electronic waste, they play likewise had an impact in manageability endeavors. Digitalization has decreased the requirement for actual assets, like paper, and cell phones have empowered eco-accommodating practices like working from home, diminishing the carbon impression related with driving to work.

The effect of cell phones on society has been tremendous and diverse, and it keeps on advancing. In any case, it's fundamental to perceive that this change has not been without its difficulties and concerns.

One critical test is the issue of screen habit and its effect on emotional well-being. The steady network and the bait of web-based entertainment have raised worries about cell phone habit, prompting issues like diminished efficiency, nervousness, and upset rest designs. Tracking down a good overall arrangement between computerized life and disconnected life has turned into a squeezing worry for some.

Protection and security are additionally central worries in the cell phone time. The broad assortment of individual information by tech organizations, the potential for information breaks, and observation have brought up issues about individual security and the requirement for powerful information insurance guidelines.

The advanced separation is another issue that has arisen. While cell phones have brought mind boggling availability and data access, not every person has equivalent admittance to these advancements. Differences in cell phone proprietorship and web access endure, leaving a few networks in a tough spot.

Also, the dispensable idea of cell phones has natural ramifications. The creation, utilization, and removal of electronic gadgets add to electronic waste (e-squander) and natural corruption. Feasible practices in cell phone assembling and reusing are fundamental for alleviating these effects.

In the domain of advanced prosperity, worries about the impacts of screen time on kids' improvement have prompted conversations about age-proper cell phone use and parental controls. There is a developing consciousness of the need to adjust youngsters' admittance to cell phones with different types of play and learning.

The cell phone's effect on our capacities to focus and mental capacities has likewise been a subject of discussion. With a steady stream of warnings and data readily available, our capacity to concentrate and participate in profound, supported speculation might reduce.

1.2 The rise of video applications and their significance in the digital age

In the consistently developing scene of the computerized age, video applications have arisen as a predominant power, reshaping how we consume, make, and communicate with visual substance. These applications, which range a wide range from virtual entertainment stages to real time features, have essentially modified the manner in which we draw in with video content. The ascent of video applications is a multi-layered peculiarity, set apart by significant changes by they way we engage ourselves, interface with others, get data, and express our inventiveness. In this conversation, we will investigate the development of video applications and their sweeping importance in the advanced age.

The starting points of video applications can be followed back to the beginning of the web when the capacity to share and view recordings online was an original idea. The mid 2000s saw the rise of stages like YouTube, which permitted clients to transfer, offer, and view recordings on a worldwide scale. These stages democratized content creation, leading to a time of client produced content. At first, the substance differed broadly in quality, going from beginner home recordings to imaginative undertakings, yet the idea of video-sharing was conceived.

The appearance of high velocity web, better video pressure calculations, and the expansion of advanced gadgets with video capacities prepared for the unstable development of video applications. The ascent of cell phones furnished with top notch cameras and the accessibility of quick 4G and 5G organizations further sped up this pattern. Thus, video applications have turned into an indispensable piece of our computerized lives, including a wide exhibit of functionalities and use cases.

One of the critical drivers of the prevalence of video applications is the comfort they offer. With a cell phone close by, clients can now convey whole libraries of movies, Programs, and recordings, open whenever, in any spot. The accommodation of on-request video web-based features has changed our review propensities, permitting us to watch what we need, when we need it. Marathon watching whole times of most loved series or getting up to speed with missed episodes of Network programs has turned into a social peculiarity, empowered by video applications. Conventional TV timetables and channel limitations have given approach to customized, adaptable survey encounters.

Moreover, the personalization and proposal calculations utilized by video applications have improved our drenching in satisfied. These calculations tackle the force of large information and AI to arrange content in light of our inclinations, seeing history, and segment data. They assist clients with finding new happy as well as make protected, closed off environments where people are presented to data and media that line up with their current convictions and interests. This

personalization can have both positive and pessimistic results, as it can improve our client experience by acquainting us with content we probably won't have in any case experienced, however it can likewise prompt data air pockets and channel bubbles that support our current predispositions and breaking point our openness to different viewpoints.

The vivid idea of video applications additionally stretches out past diversion to incorporate instruction. With the coming of huge open web-based courses (MOOCs) and e-learning stages, cell phone clients can get to an abundance of instructive substance readily available. These stages offer courses, talks, and instructional exercises on a large number of subjects, empowering deep rooted mastering and abilities improvement. The adaptability and availability of cell phone based instruction have democratized getting the hang of, making it workable for people all over the planet to obtain information and abilities that were once restricted to conventional instructive establishments.

Also, the intuitiveness and commitment of video applications have changed how we associate with instructive substance. Gamification, intelligent tests, and conversation gatherings inside these applications make learning more captivating as well as take into consideration evaluation and input, upgrading the general opportunity for growth. Thus, the cell phone has turned into an incredible asset for both conventional training and independent learning, with the possibility to connect instructive holes and enable people to seek after their scholarly and proficient goals.

While video applications offer accommodation and personalization, they likewise bring up significant issues about how they shape our social communications. The pervasiveness of cell phones and online entertainment stages has changed the manner in which we convey and associate with others. Video calls, live web based, and stories have become essential parts of our computerized collaborations, empowering us to see and be found progressively. Video applications give a stage to sharing individual encounters, sentiments, and inventive articulations, encouraging a feeling of having a place and network that rises above geological limits.

The ascent of video applications has likewise re-imagined the idea of "powerhouses" and VIPs. People who gain unmistakable quality through stages like YouTube, Instagram, and TikTok can gather huge followings and apply critical impact over their crowd. These advanced characters frequently obscure the lines among legitimacy and execution, introducing painstakingly created personas that can be adapted through brand organizations and supports. The power and reach of these forces to be reckoned with have disturbed conventional publicizing models, as brands perceive the worth of powerhouse advertising in interfacing with more youthful and all the more carefully canny crowds. This, thus, has led to conversations about straightforwardness, credibility, and the obligations of powerhouses in molding public discernments and ways of behaving.

The omnipresence of video applications additionally presents critical difficulties and open doors for news and reporting. While these applications give a stage to quick news dispersal and resident reporting, they have likewise led to worries about the spread of deception, counterfeit news, and channel bubbles. The speed at which data goes through video applications can enhance the effect of bits of hearsay and bogus stories, making it progressively challenging to observe truth from fiction. In this time of computerized data, media education has turned into a basic expertise, as clients should explore a scene where news and diversion frequently join, testing conventional thoughts of objectivity and editorial uprightness.

The impact of video applications has molded the scene of the promoting business. As customary promotion designs, like TV plugs and print notices, have become less compelling in catching buyers' consideration, sponsors have gone to video applications for the purpose of arriving at their interest groups. In-stream promotions, supported content, and powerhouse coordinated efforts have become normal techniques for brands to draw in with customers. Moreover, information examination and focusing on apparatuses permit sponsors to fit their messages to explicit socioeconomics, further obscuring the lines among content and publicizing. This has raised worries about client protection, information security, and the moral ramifications of information driven promoting rehearses.

The connection between video applications and psychological wellbeing is a subject of developing concern. The consistent openness to screens, the habit-forming nature of virtual entertainment looking over, and the tensions related with online self-show can prompt issues like advanced compulsion, nervousness, and wretchedness. These worries have incited conversations about computerized detox, care, and dependable screen using time productively, as people endeavor to track down a harmony between their advanced and disconnected lives.

Past individual clients, the submersion in video applications has more extensive cultural ramifications. It has changed how we draw in with legislative issues, as virtual entertainment stages and live-streaming have become devices for political activation, activism, and mindfulness. The fast dispersal of recordings portraying social and political occasions significantly affects public talk, impacting the manner in which we see and answer issues like civil rights, basic freedoms, and natural worries.

In addition, the impact of video applications has formed the scene of the amusement and content creation businesses. Customary media organizations, when the guardians of amusement, are currently rivaling computerized local stages for crowd consideration. The ascent of client produced content has enabled people to become content makers, testing the customary progressive system of media creation. This democratization of content creation has prompted the development of different voices and stories, however it has likewise raised worries about copyright encroachment, licensed innovation, and the maintainability of inventive professions.

As the combination of video applications into our lives keeps on extending, the idea of security is going through a significant change. The consistent network of cell phones, the assortment of individual information, and the potential for reconnaissance have raised worries about the disintegration of security. The compromise among comfort and individual information security has prompted banters about the requirement for more grounded information insurance guidelines and the moral utilization of individual data.

All in all, the submersion of cell phone clients in video applications is a diverse peculiarity that has reshaped the manner in which we engage, teach, impart, and communicate with the world. The comfort, personalization, and intuitiveness of these applications have altered our advanced encounters, empowering us to convey whole libraries of content, take part in deep rooted learning, and associate with others in manners that were once unbelievable. Nonetheless, this change isn't without its difficulties, as it brings up issues about the effect on psychological wellness, the spread of deception.

Chapter 2

The Allure of Video Content

Video content has unquestionably turned into a characterizing part of our lives in the 21st hundred years. From the beginning of TV to the advanced time of web-based features, recordings have developed and adjusted to meet our consistently changing requirements and wants. The appeal of video content is discernible, attracting us with its dazzling visuals, convincing narrating, and the strong capacity to pass on data and feelings. In this computerized age, video content has risen above limits and turned into a pervasive medium that impacts our way of life, correspondence, and, surprisingly, our day to day schedules.

One of the most major explanations behind the appeal of video content is its visual nature. Individuals are innately visual animals. Our cerebrums are wired to deal with visual data more productively than text or sound alone. Video content profits by this inborn inclination by giving a tactile encounter that draws in various faculties at the same time. The mix of moving pictures, varieties, and sound makes a multisensory experience that catches our consideration and makes the substance more vital. Whether it's a stunning nature narrative, an outright exhilarating activity film, or an educational instructional exercise, video content has a remarkable capacity to drench the watcher in the story, moving them to various universes and encounters.

Besides, video content offers a unique stage for narrating. It permits makers to create accounts that can be wealthy exhaustively, feeling, and intricacy. The capacity to consolidate exchange, music, embellishments, and cinematography makes video an inconceivably adaptable vehicle for narrating. From the grasping show of a Shakespearean play to the comedic virtuoso of a sitcom, video content can convey stories that resound with a different scope of crowds. It rises above language and social obstructions, making it a general instrument for conveying human encounters and feelings.

The appeal of video content is additionally intently attached to its capacity to actually pass on data. During a time where data is promptly accessible and capacities to focus are diminishing, video content gives a brief and drawing in method for correspondence. Whether it's a TED Talk, a narrative on a verifiable occasion, or an informative cooking video, the mix of visuals and verbally expressed words can improve on complex ideas and upgrade perception. This is particularly significant in schooling, as video content has changed the manner in which we learn. From online courses to instructive YouTube channels, video content has made learning more open, drawing in, and intuitive.

The ascent of online entertainment stages has additionally intensified the appeal of video content. Stages like YouTube, Instagram, TikTok, and Facebook have led to another age of content makers. Anybody with a cell phone and a web association can turn into a video content maker, sharing their encounters, abilities, and innovativeness with a world-wide crowd. This democratization of content creation has prompted the expansion of video content, with specialty networks conforming to different interests and interests. From magnificence instructional exercises to gaming live streams, these stages have become strong vehicles for self-articulation and local area building.

Notwithstanding private substance creation, virtual entertainment stages have likewise altered the manner in which organizations and brands communicate with purchasers. Video content is presently a basic piece of promoting and publicizing systems. Brands make dazzling video notices to get the notice of likely clients, recount their image story, and lay out a profound association. The charm of video content lies in its capacity to convey the embodiment of a brand or item in a limited capacity to focus time, leaving an enduring effect on the crowd.

Live video real time has added another aspect to the charm of video content. Stages like Jerk and YouTube Live have led to a flourishing society of live gaming, where players can communicate their ongoing interaction to a live crowd. This not just permits gamers to interface with their fans yet in addition acquaints an intuitive component with the review insight. Watchers can remark, seek clarification on pressing issues, and even impact the game being played, making a feeling of local area and investment.

Additionally, live streaming has extended past gaming. It has turned into a stage for live occasions, from shows and sports to news inclusion and meetings. The continuous idea of live streaming adds a component of unconventionality and fervor, making it an appealing mode for the two makers and crowds. Live video content considers quick criticism and commitment, cultivating a feeling of association that conventional pre-recorded content can't repeat.

The allure of video content is additionally interlaced with its comfort and availability. The expansion of cell phones and rapid web has made it more straightforward than at any other time to get to video content in a hurry. Whether it's streaming a film during a drive, watching an instructional exercise while preparing supper, or getting up to speed with the most recent news in bed, video content fits consistently into our day to day schedules. The on-request nature of video real time features like Netflix, Amazon Prime, and Disney+ implies that we can watch what we need, when we need, without being attached to a particular transmission plan.

Video content's pervasiveness isn't restricted to diversion; it has turned into a key device for different areas, including reporting and activism. The instantaneousness and visual effect of video make it a strong mode for recording and sharing certifiable occasions. As of late, we have seen the impact of video content in molding general assessment and considering people with great influence responsible. The boundless utilization of cell phones with video recording abilities has made it workable for people to catch and share film of significant occasions, from political fights to cases of police mercilessness.

While video content's appeal is verifiable, it isn't without its difficulties. The sheer volume of video content accessible can be overpowering, and it's not difficult to tumble down a deep, dark hole of vast recordings, prompting issues of using time effectively and data over-burden. Also, worries about screen time and its effect on physical and emotional well-being have been raised, especially comparable to youngsters and teenagers. It is fundamental for find some kind of harmony between the advantages of video content and its possible disadvantages, and to be aware of our utilization propensities.

The charm of video content has suggestions for content makers and ventures the same. The interest for excellent video creation has flooded, setting out open doors for movie producers, videographers, artists, and different experts in the field. As organizations and brands put more in video showcasing, there is a developing requirement for imaginative people who can deliver connecting with and compelling video content. The ascent of web-based features has likewise changed media outlets, prompting a flood in unique substance creation and the making of new position open doors in the area.

Besides, the appeal of video content has reshaped the manner in which we consume news and data. Conventional print media and even TV news have needed to adjust to the evolving scene. Numerous media sources currently focus on computerized video content to contact more extensive and more different crowds. The visual and profound effect of video can make reports seriously convincing and appealing, further impacting popular assessment and talk.

The appeal of video content has additionally achieved new difficulties in the domain of advanced proficiency and decisive reasoning. With the ascent of deepfake innovation, the differentiation among true and controlled video content has become progressively challenging to observe. This calls for media proficiency schooling to assist people with exploring the advanced scene, basically assess the substance they experience, and recognize solid and problematic sources.

Video content is a dynamic and developing medium. As innovation keeps on propelling, we can expect further advancements that will shape the eventual fate of video content. Computer generated reality (VR) and expanded reality (AR) are now doing something worth remembering, offering vivid and intuitive encounters that go past conventional video. These advancements can possibly reclassify narrating, schooling, and diversion.

2.1 The variety of video content available on smartphone apps.

Cell phone applications have generally had an impact on the manner in which we consume video content. The omnipresence of cell phones, high velocity web, and a huge number of applications have made it simpler than any time in recent memory to get to an immense and different exhibit of video content. From short-structure diversion to instructive substance and virtual entertainment recordings, the assortment of video content accessible on cell phone applications is faltering. This change in the manner we draw in with video content has achieved critical changes by they way we engage ourselves, learn, and associate with others.

The ascent of web-based entertainment stages plays had a critical impact in the multiplication of video content on cell phones. Applications like Instagram, TikTok, and Snapchat have re-imagined how we share and consume short, captivating recordings. These stages have led to another type of content, where quickness is critical, and innovativeness flourishes. Clients can post recordings that reach from a couple of moments to several minutes, offering speedy looks into their lives, humor, gifts, and inventiveness. The charm of these stages lies in their capacity to convey scaled down diversion, making it simple for clients to look at a consistent transfer of recordings and remain locked in. TikTok, specifically, has turned into a worldwide peculiarity, offering a stage for clients to make, share, and find brief recordings set up with a good soundtrack.

This configuration has not just changed the manner in which we collaborate with video content however has likewise birthed new web big names and patterns. Viral difficulties, dance frenzies, and images frequently start on these stages, fanning out like quickly and molding mainstream society. The assortment of content on these applications is enormous, taking special care of a large number of interests, from parody and dance to cooking and design. Clients can easily share their own manifestations or basically be engaged by the inventiveness of others.

Also, online entertainment applications have coordinated live streaming elements, permitting clients to communicate themselves progressively, sharing encounters, occasions, and extraordinary minutes with their devotees. Live streaming has turned into an incredible asset for building networks, as watchers can communicate with telecasters through remarks and likes, cultivating a feeling of association and cooperation.

One more huge class of video content accessible on cell phone applications is instructive substance. With the coming of applications like YouTube and instructive stages like Khan Foundation, Coursera, and edX, anybody with a cell phone and a web association can get to an abundance of information. Instructive video content traverses a wide range, from informative instructional exercises to far reaching courses.

YouTube, specifically, has developed into a huge store of instructive material. Clients can track down instructional exercises on a great many subjects, from figuring out how to play an instrument to dominating another dialect or leveling up specialized abilities. The configuration of video takes into consideration clear and visual clarifications, making it a favored vehicle for grasping complex ideas. Instructive substance makers, frequently alluded to as "EduTubers," have acquired prevalence by giving drawing in and useful recordings on different subjects. This democratization of instruction has made learning more open and intelligent, as clients can draw in with content at their own speed and as per their own advantages.

For those searching for more proper schooling, applications like Coursera, Khan Foundation, and edX offer courses from colleges and organizations around the world. These applications empower clients to get to top notch schooling, frequently for nothing or for a portion of the expense of conventional educational cost. The adaptability of portable learning makes it feasible for people to seek after degrees and certificates from esteemed establishments without the need to move or focus on an unbending class plan.

News and data utilization have likewise been upset by cell phone applications. Customary print media and TV have needed to adjust to the changing computerized scene. News applications from significant outlets like The New York Times, BBC, and CNN give moment admittance to making it known stories, articles, and video content. The visual effect of video improves the news utilization experience, making occasions and stories really captivating and interesting. Clients can watch video clasps of information portions, meetings, and narratives straightforwardly on their cell phones, permitting them to remain informed any place they are.

In addition, web-based entertainment stages have become critical wellsprings of information. Numerous clients go to stages like Twitter and Facebook to get to ongoing updates and video content connected with recent developments. Resident reporting has acquired conspicuousness, as people catch and offer video film of significant occasions, from catastrophic events to fights. Video content, in this unique circumstance, fills in as an integral asset for documentation, activism, and demonstrating the veracity of history.

Media outlets has not been safe to the cell phone application unrest. Real time features like Netflix, Amazon Prime Video, Disney+, and Hulu have reclassified the manner in which we watch motion pictures and network shows. These applications give admittance to a tremendous library of content that can be streamed straightforwardly to our cell phones, presenting on-request diversion that fits consistently into our everyday schedules. The range of kinds and content accessible is faltering, from exemplary movies and gorge commendable television series to unique substance delivered solely for these stages.

Also, real time features have put vigorously in unique substance creation. This has prompted a flood in great series and films that take care of different preferences and inclinations. The accessibility of content on cell phone applications implies that clients can convey their number one shows and films with them any place they go. This has likewise led to the peculiarity of "marathon watching," where watchers consume numerous episodes or a whole time of a show at a time. The comfort of versatile streaming has changed what we engage ourselves as well as meant for how content is delivered and conveyed.

Music streaming applications like Spotify and Apple Music have correspondingly modified how we appreciate music. Clients can get to a tremendous inventory of tunes, playlists, and collections, making customized music libraries that are promptly accessible on their cell phones. Music recordings, when basically circulated on TV, can now be transferred on stages like YouTube and Vevo, straightforwardly on cell phones. The coordination of music and video upgrades the music listening experience, permitting clients to draw in with their number one specialists outwardly as well as detectably.

Gaming applications have likewise experienced huge development, offering many encounters for gamers of all levels and interests. From relaxed portable games to reassure quality titles, cell phone applications have turned into a strong stage for gaming. Easygoing games like "Treats Pound" and "Irate Birds" have drawn in large number of players, offering speedy and engaging redirections during spare minutes. Notwithstanding, versatile gaming isn't restricted to basic, time-killing encounters. Games like "Fortnite" and "PlayerUnknown's Landmarks (PUBG)" have exhibited that perplexing and vivid gaming encounters can be effectively ported to cell phones, offering console-like gaming in a hurry.

The ascent of expanded reality (AR) and computer generated reality (VR) has acquainted completely new aspects with video content accessible on cell phone applications. AR applications, as Pokémon GO, have charmed clients by mixing the virtual and actual universes. Clients can investigate their certifiable environmental factors while communicating with computerized components, making creative and intuitive encounters. VR applications, then again, offer vivid 3D conditions that transport clients to altogether new domains. These applications are utilized for gaming, reenactments, and even treatment.

Video content on cell phone applications has likewise tracked down its spot in the realm of wellness and prosperity. Applications like Nike Preparing Club and MyFitnessPal offer different exercise recordings and wellness schedules that can be gotten to from the center of your hand. These applications have made it simpler for people to remain dynamic and focus on their wellbeing, with video content filling in as a fitness coach and inspiration.

The fleeting ascent of podcasting has not slipped through the cracks, as numerous applications, similar to Apple Webcasts and Spotify, offer broad libraries of sound substance. Be that as it may, video webcasts have additionally acquired prevalence, giving watchers the choice to watch digital recording episodes rather than simply tuning in. This intermingling of sound and video has made another road for content makers and a more vivid encounter for purchasers.

The charm of video content accessible on cell phone applications lies in its accommodation, variety, and openness. Whether you're looking for diversion, schooling, news, or a blend of these, there's an application or a few applications custom fitted to your necessities. The capacity to consume video content in a hurry, at your own speed, and on a gadget that fits in your pocket has changed the manner in which we cooperate with the world and one another. Besides, it has democratized content creation, permitting people and organizations to share their accounts, mastery, and inventiveness with a worldwide crowd.

Notwithstanding its many benefits, the developing pervasiveness of video content on cell phone applications additionally raises significant contemplations. Worries about screen time and its effect on physical and psychological well-being have come to the front. The habit-forming nature of looking at perpetual video content can prompt issues of using time productively and data over-burden. It's crucial for find some kind of harmony between the advantages of video content and its possible disadvantages and to be aware of our utilization propensities.

The ascent of short-structure, exceptionally visual substance has additionally led to worries about the effect of these stages on client psychological well-being, especially among youthful crowds. The consistent examination with organized and frequently glorified web-based lives can prompt insecurities, nervousness, and gloom. Online entertainment stages and content makers are progressively being tested to make more dependable and careful substance.

Protection and information security are other critical worries with regards to cell phone applications that offer video content. Clients frequently give individual data and information to get to these applications, bringing up issues about how that data is dealt with and utilized. Late discussions encompassing information breaks and protection infringement have featured the requirement for better defends and straightforwardness around here.

All in all, the assortment of video content accessible on cell phone applications has altered the manner in which we engage ourselves, learn, and associate with others. These applications have made it workable for anybody with a cell phone and a web association with access an inconceivable cluster of content, from short, captivating virtual entertainment recordings to far reaching instructive courses. The cell phone has turned into a compact amusement and training center point, it is both different and open to convey content that. While this change has brought various advantages, it additionally presents difficulties connected with screen time, psychological wellness, protection, and information security. As we keep on exploring the developing scene of video content on cell phone applications, it's crucial for outfit its power for positive effect while staying watchful in tending to its possible downsides.

2.2 How video content captivates and engages users.

Video content has arisen as one of the most spellbinding and connecting with types of media in the computerized age. Whether it's brief video cuts via virtual entertainment, inside and out narratives, or instructive instructional exercises, video content has an interesting skill to hold our consideration, summon feelings, and pass on data. Its ability to enthrall and connect with clients is driven by a blend of variables, including its visual allure, narrating potential, and intelligence. This article investigates how video content achieves this and why it has become such a prevailing power in the web-based world.

Visual Allure: The Force of Moving Pictures

One of the essential purposes for the enrapturing idea of video content is its visual allure. Individuals are innately attracted to moving pictures. Our minds are wired to handle visual data more proficiently than text or static pictures. This visual inclination is profoundly imbued in our developmental history. For millennia, our progenitors depended on their capacity to recognize movement and changes in their current circumstance to make due.

Video content use this inborn inclination by giving a multisensory experience. It joins moving pictures with variety, sound, and frequently music to make a vivid and drawing in tactile bundle. The unique idea of video, with its changing scenes and groupings, keeps our minds effectively handling data. This catches our consideration as well as upgrades our memorable capacity and review the substance. Subsequently, whether it's a dazzling nature narrative, an activity pressed film, or a spellbinding instructive video, the visual allure of video content is certain.

Narrating Potential: Making Profound Associations

One more vital part of video content's spellbinding nature is its narrating potential. Video is a medium that permits makers to create stories wealthy exhaustively, feeling, and intricacy. Through the blend of discourse, music, embellishments, and cinematography, video content can bring out a large number of feelings, from delight and fervor to bitterness and compassion.

Stories in video content frequently follow a three-act structure, presenting characters, laying everything out, and working to a peak and goal. This design, got from the universe of theater and film, fills in as a strong diagram for charming narrating.

The capacity to pass stories on through video isn't restricted to conventional movies or network shows. In the time of short-structure content on stages like TikTok and Instagram, makers have become proficient at recounting to miniature stories in only a couple of moments. These scaled down accounts catch the substance of a story in a minimized and drawing in design, reverberating with watchers who have restricted time or capacities to focus.

The force of narrating in video content isn't restricted to fiction. Narratives, for example, utilize the narrating arrangement to investigate certifiable occasions, verifiable records, and instructive subjects. The close to home association that video content can lay out with watchers frequently prompts a more profound comprehension and maintenance of the substance.

Intuitiveness: Encouraging Watcher Interest

Video content's capacity to spellbind and connect with clients goes past detached review. Numerous video stages, particularly on the web, offer intuitive elements that consider watcher support and commitment. These intuitive components effectively make a feeling of local area and contribution, further improving the enthralling idea of video content.

One remarkable illustration of this intuitiveness is found in live web based stages like Jerk and YouTube Live. Gamers and content makers utilize these stages to communicate their interactivity, offer live critique, and collaborate with their crowd progressively. Watchers can remark, get clarification on pressing issues, and even impact the interactivity, making a feeling of shared insight and local area. This live cooperation cultivates an association between the substance maker and the crowd that goes past customary media's one-way correspondence.

Also, live streaming has extended past gaming. It has turned into a stage for live occasions, like shows, sports, and news inclusion. The quickness and continuous nature of live streaming add a component of capriciousness and fervor that is hard to duplicate in prerecorded content.

Intuitive video content isn't restricted to live streaming. Indeed, even prerecorded recordings can consolidate components like interactive connections, reviews, or intuitive explanations that permit watchers to draw in with the substance. Instructive recordings, specifically, frequently utilize intelligent highlights to test watchers, give extra assets, or brief conversations.

Availability and Accommodation: Content Readily available

The openness and comfort of video content likewise assume a critical part in its charming nature. The expansion of cell phones and fast web has made it more straightforward than any time in recent memory to get to video content whenever and anyplace. The on-request nature of video web-based features, for example, Netflix, Amazon Prime Video, and YouTube, permits watchers to watch what they need, when they need, without being attached to a particular transmission plan.

Cell phones have turned into the essential gadget for video utilization. With their high-goal screens and compactness, they give an ideal stage to survey video content. Whether it's watching a film during a drive, following an instructional exercise while cooking, or getting up to speed with the most recent news in bed, video content consistently coordinates into our everyday schedules.

The variety of content accessible on cell phones is shocking. From short online entertainment recordings to full length films, and from instructive instructional exercises to live streams, the scope of content takes special care of an expansive range of interests and inclinations. The capacity to access such a wide assortment of content on a solitary gadget upgrades the comfort and enamoring nature of video content.

Democratization of Content Creation: Everybody Can Be a Maker

The charming idea of video content isn't exclusively capable by watchers. It is likewise a main thrust behind the democratization of content creation. In the computerized age, anybody with a cell phone and a web association can turn into a substance maker, delivering recordings that catch their encounters, abilities, and imagination.

Web-based entertainment stages, particularly YouTube, have been instrumental in engaging people to share their abilities and interests. Whether it's cosmetics instructional exercises, touring video blogs, or cooking exhibitions, people from around the world can make and share content that resounds with a worldwide crowd. The charm of video content creation lies in the possibility to communicate one's thoughts, construct an individual brand, and draw in with similar watchers.

This democratization of content creation has brought about the arrangement of specialty networks around different interests. Magnificence fans can interface through cosmetics instructional exercises, gamers can bond over live streams, and specialists can impart their tasks to a committed following. These people group offer a feeling of having a place and shared enthusiasm, further extending the commitment with video content.

Influence on Business and Marking: Building Close to home Associations

The dazzling idea of video content has not slipped through the cracks by organizations and brands. Video showcasing and promoting have become necessary pieces of computerized advertising procedures. Brands make enthralling video ads to get the notice of likely clients, convey their image story, and lay out a close to home association. The charm of video content lies in its capacity to convey the quintessence of a brand or item in a limited ability to focus time, leaving an enduring effect on the crowd.

Profound associations assume a critical part in the viability of video publicizing. A very much created video can possibly summon a great many feelings, from giggling and sentimentality to motivation and compassion. These close to home associations can essentially impact shopper conduct, prompting expanded brand steadfastness and deals.

Besides, narrating is a common methodology in video promoting. Brands use narrating to make stories that resound with their main interest group. These accounts adapt the brand, making it interesting and essential. By meshing stories into their promoting endeavors, organizations can draw in with purchasers on a more profound level.

The ascent of powerhouses and content makers has additionally changed the scene of brand showcasing. Forces to be reckoned with frequently have a devoted and drawn in crowd, making them strong brand diplomats. Cooperating with powerhouses permits brands to take advantage of the trust and compatibility that powerhouses have worked with their adherents.

The Ascent of Online Entertainment and Short-Structure Content

Web-based entertainment stages play had a huge impact in reshaping the scene of video content. Applications like Instagram, TikTok, and Snapchat have led to short-shape video content, which has turned into a predominant power in catching and holding client consideration.

These stages focus on curtness, with recordings that can go from a couple of moments to two or three minutes. The configuration is intended for fast and drawing in utilization, ideal for clients with restricted time or limited capacity to focus. The allure of short-structure video content lies in its capacity to convey an eruption of diversion or data in a reduced and effectively edible bundle.

TikTok, specifically, has arisen as a worldwide peculiarity, offering a stage for clients to make, share, and find brief recordings set up with a good soundtrack. The stage's calculation driven content revelation and virality have pursued it a favored decision for clients looking for fast, engaging, and frequently comical video content. TikTok's prosperity is credited to its capacity to comprehend client inclinations and present a customized feed of recordings that reverberate with every client.

The short-structure video design has led to another age of web superstars and patterns. Viral difficulties, dance frenzies, and images frequently begin on these stages, spreading quickly and impacting mainstream society. The drawing in nature of short-structure content is a demonstration of its capacity to charm and hold client consideration in a universe of consistent interruptions.

The Appeal of Instructive Video Content

Instructive video content has seen huge development lately, and its enrapturing nature is driven by its capacity to make picking up drawing in and available. Stages like YouTube, Khan Foundation, Coursera, and edX have changed how we access instructive material.

YouTube, specifically, has developed into a tremendous vault of instructive substance. Clients can track down instructional exercises on a great many subjects, from figuring out how to play an instrument to dominating another dialect or improving specialized abilities. The visual and hear-able components of video content make it a compelling mode for improving on complex ideas and upgrading understanding.

Instructive substance makers, frequently alluded to as "EduTubers," have acquired ubiquity by giving connecting with and educational recordings on different subjects. Their capacity to separate points and make sense of them outwardly helps students of any age and foundations. The democratization of schooling through video content has made learning more intelligent, independent, and versatile to individual requirements.

For those looking for more organized and formal instruction, stages like Coursera, Khan Foundation, and edX offer courses from colleges and organizations around the world. These applications permit clients to get to great schooling, frequently free of charge or for a portion of the expense of conventional educational cost. The adaptability of portable learning makes it workable for people to seek after degrees and accreditations from esteemed foundations without the need to move or stick to unbending class plans.

The Impact of Live Video Web based

Live video web based has added another aspect to the spellbinding idea of video content. Stages like Jerk and YouTube Live have led to a flourishing society of live gaming, where players can communicate their interactivity to a live crowd.

Live streaming offers watchers a novel and intuitive experience. They can remark, clarify pressing issues, and even impact the game being played, making a feeling of local area and investment. This live communication cultivates an association between happy makers and their crowd that goes past conventional media.

Moreover, live streaming isn't restricted to gaming. It has extended to incorporate live occasions, for example, shows, sports matches, and news inclusion. The ongoing idea of live streaming adds a component of flightiness and fervor, making it an appealing mechanism for the two makers and crowds. The capacity to give quick criticism and participate continuously conversations encourages a feeling of local area and shared insight.

Openness and Comfort in Video Content Utilization

The openness and accommodation of video content have contributed altogether to its enthralling nature. Cell phones have turned into the essential gadget for video utilization. With high-goal screens, transportability, and a consistent web association, cell phones offer an ideal stage for watching video content. This availability implies that clients can appreciate video content for all intents and purposes anyplace, whenever.

The variety of content accessible on cell phones is broad, going from short web-based entertainment recordings to full length films and from instructive instructional exercises to live streams. This assortment takes care of a wide range of interests and inclinations, further upgrading the comfort and enthralling nature of video content.

Video real time features, for example, Netflix, Amazon Prime Video, and Disney+, have changed how we consume amusement. These applications offer on-request admittance to a broad library of content, permitting watchers to watch what they need when they need. The comfort of versatile streaming has had an impact on the manner in which we engage ourselves as well as affected the creation and circulation of content.

Music streaming applications, as Spotify and Apple Music, have correspondingly reshaped how we appreciate music. Clients can get to an immense inventory of melodies, playlists, and collections, making customized music libraries promptly accessible on their cell phones. Music recordings, when basically broadcasted on TV, can now be transferred on stages like YouTube and Vevo, straightforwardly on cell phones. This incorporation of music and video improves the music-listening experience, permitting clients to draw in with their number one specialists outwardly as well as detectably.

Gaming applications have likewise experienced critical development, offering a great many encounters for gamers of all levels and interests. From easygoing portable games to comfort quality titles, cell phone applications have turned into a strong stage for gaming. This openness has made gaming a piece of day to day existence for some people, offering fast and drawing in diversion at whatever point there's an extra second.

The omnipresence of video content available through cell phones has changed how we consume news and data. Conventional news sources, like papers and TV news, have adjusted to the computerized scene by offering applications that give moment admittance to articles and video content. The visual effect of video improves the news utilization experience, making occasions and stories really captivating and appealing. Clients can watch video clasps of information fragments, meetings, and narratives straightforwardly on their cell phones, permitting them to remain informed any place they are.

Virtual entertainment stages have likewise become huge wellsprings of information and data. Numerous clients go to stages like Twitter and

Facebook for continuous updates and video content connected with recent developments. The far reaching utilization of cell phones with video recording abilities has made it feasible for people to catch and share film of significant occasions, from catastrophic events to fights. Video content has turned into an amazing asset for documentation, activism, and taking the stand concerning history.

The Difficulties and Contemplations

While video content's spellbinding nature is clear, it isn't without its difficulties and contemplations. The sheer volume of video content accessible can be overpowering, prompting issues of using time productively and data over-burden. The steady accessibility of video content on cell phones can make it simple to tumble down a deep, dark hole of vast recordings, possibly influencing efficiency and prosperity.

Besides, worries about screen time and its effect on physical and emotional wellness have been raised, especially according to kids and young people. Extreme screen time can prompt issues like computerized eye strain, upset rest designs, and an inactive way of life. Finding a harmony between the advantages of video content and the potential downsides is significant for keeping a solid way of life in the computerized age.

Likewise, the ascent of deepfake innovation has confounded the scene of video content. Deepfakes are profoundly persuading controlled recordings that can cause it to seem like people are saying or doing things they won't ever do. The qualification among valid and controlled video content has become progressively challenging to recognize. This has raised worries about falsehood, security, and the potential for hurt.

Media education and decisive reasoning abilities have become more significant than any other time in recent memory in the computerized age. It is fundamental to instruct people about how to explore the advanced scene, basically assess the substance they experience, and recognize dependable and problematic sources. These abilities are essential for settling on informed choices, both as buyers and makers of video content.

The Effect on Businesses and Work

The charming idea of video content significantly affects different businesses and has set out new work open doors. The interest for top notch video creation has flooded, prompting potential open doors for movie producers, videographers, illustrators, and different experts in the field. As organizations and brands put more in video promoting, there is a developing requirement for imaginative people who can create drawing in and compelling video content. The ascent of real time features has likewise changed media outlets, prompting a flood in unique substance creation and the formation of new position valuable open doors in the area.

The news business has needed to adjust to the changing computerized scene, with video content assuming a critical part. Numerous media sources currently focus on advanced video content to contact more extensive and more assorted crowds. Video reports and narratives have become instrumental in molding popular assessment and talk. Writers and media experts who can deliver convincing video content are popular.

Besides, the democratization of content creation has prompted the ascent of forces to be reckoned with and content makers as powerful figures in different ventures, from magnificence and design to gaming and innovation. These makers frequently work together with brands and organizations, turning out to be strong powerhouses in their particular specialties. The powerhouse promoting industry has developed considerably, offering new business amazing open doors for powerhouses, administrators, and advertisers.

Chapter 3

The Portability Revolution

The 21st century has seen an exceptional change in the manner we connect with innovation. From the coming of the web to the multiplication of cell phones and the ascent of wearable gadgets, our reality has become progressively versatile. This compactness upheaval has changed the gadgets we use as well as the manner in which we live, work, and associate with each other. In this investigation of the transportability upset, we will dig into the historical backdrop of compact innovation, the effect it has had on different parts of our lives, and the potential future improvements that look for us.

The Verifiable Advancement of Compactness

The idea of compactness in innovation is certainly not a new development. It has been a piece of mankind's set of experiences for a really long time, with remarkable improvements in different spaces.

One of the earliest instances of convenient innovation can be found in the production of the math device, an old counting gadget that traces all the way back to around 2000 BCE. The math device, comprising of dabs or stones on poles, was a convenient instrument for performing number juggling computations, empowering dealers, vendors, and mathematicians to complete complex tasks.

Headways in mechanical designing led to the pocket watch in the sixteenth hundred years. These timekeeping gadgets permitted people to convey exact timekeeping systems in their pockets, essentially affecting dependability and using time effectively.

In the twentieth 100 years, the development of the versatile radio carried news and amusement to individuals' homes and permitted them to tune in a hurry. This undeniable a huge headway in compact innovation, giving admittance to data and music while staying portable.

In any case, the genuine change in the convenientce unrest accompanied the approach of individualized computing. The presentation of workstations in the late twentieth century addressed a jump forward in innovation's convenientce. These gadgets permitted people to convey strong processing instruments with them, breaking liberated from the limitations of work stations. PCs turned into the image of versatile efficiency, empowering experts to work from anyplace easily.

The following significant achievement was the rise of cell phones. These smaller gadgets, at first intended for voice correspondence, before long developed to integrate text informing, web perusing, and a great many applications. The cell phone, a blend of a cell phone and a hand-held PC, upset the manner in which we associate, access data, and do everyday errands. The send off of the main iPhone in 2007 denoted a defining moment in the conveyability transformation, as it joined different capabilities and capacities in a solitary pocket-sized gadget.

The Expansion of Cell phones

The cell phone has been at the front of the convenientce upset, reshaping the manner in which we impart, work, and communicate with the world. The effect of cell phones is diverse and has affected different parts of our regular routines.

1. **Correspondence and Network**

Cell phones have re-imagined correspondence by giving different diverts to keeping in contact with family, companions, and partners. Calls, instant messages, texting applications, and video calls have become fundamental methods of interfacing with others. The omnipresence of cell phones has made worldwide correspondence more open, lessening topographical hindrances.

Online entertainment stages, open through cell phone applications, have changed how we share and consume data. These stages have empowered clients to interface with a worldwide crowd, share their encounters, and partake in web-based networks. The capacity to post refreshes, photographs, and recordings from essentially anyplace has made it simple to remain associated with others and be important for bigger web-based networks.

2. **Work and Efficiency**

Cell phones have obscured the lines among work and individual life. With email access, archive altering devices, and undertaking the board applications, experts can stay useful in any event, when they are away from their conventional office settings. Remote work and working from home have become progressively doable, offering adaptability and balance between fun and serious activities.

Besides, the transportability of cell phones has opened up additional opportunities for consultants and business visionaries. With a cell phone and a dependable web association, people can oversee organizations, direct video gatherings, and draw in with clients from basically any area. The capacity to work remotely has re-imagined conventional work game plans and considered more decentralized and adaptable ways to deal with business.

3. **Data and Amusement**

Cell phones are entryways to an immense universe of data and diversion. With web network and a large number of applications, clients can get to news, articles, recordings, and media content on any subject of interest. The in a hurry admittance to data has changed how we consume news and remain informed about worldwide occasions.

Diversion, as well, has become progressively versatile. Music, films, and TV programs are promptly accessible through web-based features. Clients can pay attention to music, watch their number one shows, and appreciate films on their cell phones, making amusement a fundamental piece of day to day existence. The conveyability of cell phones has made long drives, travel, and margin time more pleasant and locking in.

4. **Route and Area Administrations**

Cell phones have altered route and area based administrations. GPS innovation coordinated into cell phones has made it feasible for clients to explore new spots, track down adjacent eateries, and find focal points. Area based applications offer constant traffic refreshes, public transportation data, and headings, making travel more helpful and proficient.

These applications have upgraded the movement experience for people as well as changed businesses like ride-sharing and food conveyance. Administrations like Uber and Lyft depend on GPS innovation to associate drivers with travelers, while food conveyance applications use area information to guarantee instant and precise conveyances.

5. **Photography and Self-Articulation**

The combination of excellent cameras into cell phones has made photography and self-articulation more open to a more extensive crowd. Clients can catch minutes, archive encounters, and express their innovativeness through photography and videography. Web-based entertainment stages have been instrumental in the sharing and appropriation of these visual manifestations.

The capacity to take and right away offer photographs and recordings has prompted the ascent of client produced content, adding to the democratization of media. It plays likewise had an impact in molding on the web culture, as clients participate in visual narrating, imaginative articulation, and the documentation of their lives.

6. **Wellbeing and Wellness**

The movability of cell phones has reached out to the domain of wellbeing and wellness. Wellbeing applications and wearable gadgets, frequently synchronized with cell phones, have made it simpler for people to screen their active work, track their eating routine, and deal with their wellbeing. Clients can get to exercise routine schedules, put forth wellness objectives, and get constant information on their wellbeing measurements.

These applications and gadgets have energized better ways of life and given clients the devices to assume command over their prosperity. The joining of wellness and wellbeing information into cell phone environments can possibly change how medical services is conveyed and gotten to.

Wearable Gadgets: Another Outskirts

As the versatility insurgency keeps on unfurling, wearable gadgets have arisen as another boondocks. Wearables are conservative, frequently wrist-worn gadgets that give explicit functionalities and information following. They broaden the abilities of cell phones and proposition one of a kind advantages in different spaces.

1. **Wellness and Wellbeing Checking**

   Wearable wellness trackers and smartwatches have acquired fame for their capacity to screen actual work, pulse, rest examples, and the sky is the limit from there. These gadgets give clients continuous information and bits of knowledge into their wellbeing and wellness levels, rousing them to make positive way of life changes. For people looking to keep a solid way of life, wearable gadgets offer a versatile answer for following advancement, defining objectives, and remaining inspired. The information gathered by these gadgets can be synchronized with cell phone applications, considering a far reaching outline of one's wellbeing and wellness.

2. **Upgraded Availability and Warnings**

   Smartwatches, specifically, have turned into an augmentation of the cell phone, permitting clients to get warnings, messages, and calls without taking out their telephones. This availability improves accommodation and productivity, as clients can rapidly look at their wrists to remain refreshed on significant data.

   Notwithstanding notices, smartwatches can run an assortment of applications, giving usefulness past conventional timekeeping. Clients can get to weather conditions gauges, control shrewd home gadgets, and even make portable installments with their smartwatches.

3. **Increased Reality and Computer generated Reality**

The compactness unrest has likewise brought about wearable gadgets intended for expanded reality (AR) and computer generated reality (VR) encounters. AR glasses, similar to those created by organizations like Google and Microsoft, overlay computerized data onto the actual world. Clients can get logically applicable information, headings, and intelligent encounters through these gadgets.

VR headsets, then again, transport clients to vivid virtual conditions. These gadgets are utilized for gaming, reenactments, preparing, and even treatment. The degree of submersion and intelligence in VR is unrivaled, making it an astonishing wilderness for video content, gaming, and intuitive encounters.

3.1 The convenience of smartphones and how they integrate into daily life.

The 21st century has seen a noteworthy change in the manner we live, work, and interface with each other, generally because of the boundless reception of cell phones. These little, strong gadgets have turned into a vital piece of our day to day routines, offering comfort, network, and a large number of functionalities. In this investigation of the comfort of cell phones and their consistent coordination into day to day existence, we will dive into the different parts of how these gadgets have altered our schedules, reshaped businesses, and introduced the two open doors and difficulties in the advanced age.

The Pocket-Sized Transformation

The coming of cell phones achieved a pocket-sized transformation in innovation. These gadgets are minimal, yet they pack an extraordinary measure of registering power, empowering clients to play out many undertakings in a hurry. Cell phones have developed from being straightforward specialized apparatuses to refined small PCs that are profoundly implanted in our everyday schedules.

At their center, cell phones are specialized gadgets. They permit us to settle on telephone decisions, send instant messages, and access a huge number of correspondence applications, like texting and web-based entertainment stages. During a time where network is central, these highlights are the groundwork of our interconnected world.

Nonetheless, the capacities of cell phones reach out a long ways past simple correspondence. They have become adaptable devices for efficiency, diversion, route, photography, wellbeing checking, and substantially more. Thus, the accommodation of cell phones has significantly affected our regular routines in various ways.

Smoothed out Efficiency and Network

Cell phones have changed how we work and remain useful. With email access, record altering devices, and a plenty of efficiency applications, experts can oversee errands, work together with partners, and access basic data from practically anyplace. The adaptability of cell phones has prompted the ascent of remote work and working from home, offering people more noteworthy balance between serious and fun activities and area autonomy.

Organizations have likewise saddled the capability of cell phones for promoting, client commitment, and online business. Versatile applications and sites permit organizations to interface with clients, contact more extensive crowds, and give helpful admittance to their items and administrations. The accommodation of shopping, banking, and reserving a spot through versatile applications has turned into a basic piece of current customer encounters.

Also, the appearance of video conferencing applications, similar to Zoom and Microsoft Groups, has altered the manner in which we lead gatherings and meetings. Cell phone clients can partake in video calls from any area, making distant joint effort more open than any other time in recent memory. The continuous advancement of expanded reality (AR) and augmented reality (VR) advances might much further change how we associate and connect in virtual spaces.

Amusement in a hurry

One of the most conspicuous ways cell phones have incorporated into day to day existence is by upsetting amusement. Streaming stages, for example, Netflix, Amazon Prime Video, Disney+, and different music web-based features, give admittance to a tremendous library of motion pictures, Programs, and music. Clients can partake in their number one substance during drives, while holding up in line, or in the solace of their own homes.

Portable gaming has turned into a huge wellspring of diversion, with a different scope of gaming applications accessible to clients. These applications take special care of different gaming inclinations, from relaxed games to reassure quality titles. The openness of versatile gaming has made it a fundamental piece of day to day existence for some people.

Live streaming stages, like Jerk and YouTube Live, have led to another type of amusement. Gamers, powerhouses, and content makers can communicate real time content to a worldwide crowd. Live streaming cultivates a feeling of local area among watchers, who can communicate with the substance makers progressively. It has additionally empowered the live communicating of occasions, for example, shows and sports matches, making shared encounters open through cell phones.

The allure of cell phones for amusement is additionally improved by their high-goal screens and vivid sound capacities. The gadgets offer superb visual and hear-able encounters, making them ideal for consuming a wide assortment of interactive media content.

Route and Area Administrations

Cell phones have altered how we explore and get to area based administrations. Underlying GPS innovation, combined with portable applications, empowers clients to track down bearings, find organizations, and find focal points. The times of bobbling with paper guides and requesting headings are generally behind us, because of the accommodation of GPS-prepared cell phones.

Area based applications give ongoing traffic refreshes, public transportation data, and turn-by-turn route, making travel more effective and less unpleasant. Moreover, administrations like ride-sharing and food conveyance have become vital to metropolitan living, depending on GPS innovation to interface drivers with travelers and guarantee expeditious and precise conveyances.

The accommodation of cell phone route stretches out to travel arranging and investigation. Clients can research and book flights, lodgings, and exercises from their gadgets, guaranteeing a smoother travel insight. Besides, applications like Google Guides and Apple Guides offer expanded reality includes that overlay advanced data onto the actual world, working on route much further.

Photography and Self-Articulation

Cell phones have democratized photography and self-articulation. Excellent cameras coordinated into these gadgets have made it simple for clients to catch minutes, record encounters, and express their innovativeness. Online entertainment stages play had a huge impact in the sharing and conveyance of these visual manifestations.

The capacity to take and immediately share photographs and recordings has prompted the ascent of client created content (UGC). People share their lives, experiences, and imaginative articulations with worldwide crowds, forming on the web culture and affecting patterns. UGC isn't restricted to proficient photographic artists; anybody with a cell phone can turn into a substance maker and offer their exceptional viewpoint with the world.

The combination of cameras with virtual entertainment stages has made a flourishing environment for visual narrating and self-articulation. Clients share their regular routines, travel experiences, and imaginative undertakings through photographs and recordings. The quickness and visual nature of these stages offer a drawing in and engaging method for associating with companions, family, and supporters.

Photography applications, channels, and altering instruments have additionally enabled clients to improve their visual substance and develop their own brands. The visual idea of virtual entertainment stages has made pictures and recordings vital to our internet based characters.

Wellbeing and Wellness

Cell phones have become significant apparatuses for checking wellbeing and wellness. Wellbeing applications and wearable gadgets, frequently synchronized with cell phones, permit people to follow their actual work, screen their eating routine, and deal with their wellbeing. Clients can get to gym routine schedules, put forth wellness objectives, and get constant information on their wellbeing measurements.

These applications and gadgets have supported better ways of life and given clients the devices to assume command over their prosperity. The combination of wellness and wellbeing information into cell phone biological systems can possibly reform how medical services is conveyed and gotten to. Telemedicine, for example, has become progressively available through versatile applications, permitting clients to talk with medical services experts from the solace of their homes.

Protection and Security Concerns

As cell phones have become progressively incorporated into day to day existence, worries about protection and information security have additionally risen. Clients are sharing an abundance of individual data on these gadgets, from their area and contact records to their web-based ways of behaving and inclinations. Safeguarding this information from unapproved access and guaranteeing client protection is a basic thought for the two clients and innovation organizations.

Occasions of information breaks, cyberattacks, and protection infringement have carried the issue of cell phone security to the front. Guaranteeing the security of client information and individual data is a common obligation among gadget makers, application designers, and clients. Encryption, secure validation strategies, and hearty protection settings are fundamental parts of cell phone security.

Screen Time and Advanced Prosperity

The accommodation of cell phones has prompted worries about unreasonable screen time and its effect on physical and emotional wellness. Drawn out utilization of cell phones can bring about issues like computerized eye strain, disturbed rest designs, and a stationary way of life. Tracking down a harmony between the upsides of cell phone comfort and potential disadvantages is critical for keeping a sound computerized way of life.

To address these worries, working frameworks like iOS and Android have presented screen time usage highlights. These instruments permit clients to track and restrict their screen time, put forth application explicit utilization lines, and, surprisingly, empower "Don't Upset" modes during specific hours. These highlights engage clients to assume command over their screen time and lay out better cell phone propensities.

Moral Contemplations

The mix of cell phones into day to day existence has raised moral contemplations, especially in regards to issues like computerized compulsion, online badgering, and the spread of disinformation. Innovation organizations and clients the same should be aware of the moral ramifications of their activities and the effect they have on society. Advanced proficiency, sympathy, and mindful internet based conduct are fundamental components of moral cell phone utilization.

3.2 Mobile video consumption trends.

Lately, portable video utilization has flooded, turning into a predominant power in the computerized scene. The commonness of cell phones, fast web, and the development of streaming stages has altered the manner in which we consume video content. This article dives into the versatile video utilization drifts that are molding the media scene, including the development of short-structure video, the effect on amusement and advertising, the ascent of client created content, and the difficulties and amazing open doors introduced by this quickly advancing medium.

Short-Structure Video: The Rule of Snackable Substance

Quite possibly of the main pattern in portable video utilization is the ascent of short-structure video. Short-structure recordings are normally concise, connecting with, and intended to catch and keep up with watchers' consideration in a limited capacity to focus time, frequently under a moment. Stages like TikTok and Instagram Reels have promoted this organization, giving clients a persistent feed of engaging and frequently client produced content.

The allure of short-structure video lies in its capacity to offer speedy eruptions of amusement or data. With abilities to focus decreasing in the advanced age, these brief recordings are bound to hold the watcher's advantage. Also, the upward design, enhanced for portable screens, makes short-structure recordings profoundly open and outwardly engaging on cell phones.

Makers on short-structure video stages have outfit the capability of this configuration to engage, illuminate, and even teach. They frequently depend on snappy music, imaginative altering, and connecting with narrating to establish a long term connection in no time. Subsequently, these stages have turned into a favorable place for viral difficulties, images, and patterns that spread quickly through informal communities.

The short-structure video pattern has caught the consideration of individual clients as well as drawn in organizations and publicists. Organizations are progressively utilizing these stages to contact more youthful crowds and make brand mindfulness. Short-structure recordings are a strong vehicle for conveying succinct promoting messages and drawing in with expected clients in a more customized way.

Diversion in a hurry: The Streaming Upset

The comfort and convenientce of cell phones have reshaped media outlets. Streaming stages, as Netflix, Amazon Prime Video, and Disney+, have become the overwhelming focus, offering a tremendous library of motion pictures and Television programs that clients can get to anyplace, whenever.

The development of portable video utilization has prompted a flood popular for superior grade, dynamic substance. Many real time features currently enhance their substance for versatile survey, with highlights like disconnected downloads, versatile streaming, and portable selective shows. Clients can watch their #1 motion pictures and series during their day to day drives, while holding up in line, or in the solace of their own homes.

The gaming business has likewise embraced portable video utilization. Versatile gaming applications have turned into a huge wellspring of diversion, with a great many clients getting a charge out of everything from relaxed games to reassure quality titles on their cell phones. The openness of versatile gaming has made it a fundamental piece of day to day existence for some people.

Live web based, one more branch-off of versatile video utilization, has turned into a most loved type of diversion, especially among more youthful crowds. Stages like Jerk and YouTube Live permit clients to observe live transmissions of gamers, powerhouses, and content makers. These live streams offer a constant and intelligent experience, cultivating a feeling of local area among watchers. Moreover, live occasions, for example, shows, sports matches, and news inclusion, are currently effectively available through cell phones, making it workable for clients to take part in shared encounters from any place they are.

The predominance of versatile video utilization has incited content makers to investigate new narrating strategies. Vertical video, for instance, is building up some decent momentum as a creative method for catching and draw in watchers. The upward design, planned explicitly for portable screens, permits makers to introduce content such that feels normal and vivid on cell phones. This configuration is especially well known on stages like TikTok and Instagram Stories.

Client Produced Content: The Ascent of Advanced Inventiveness

Client created content (UGC) has seen a noteworthy flood in the time of versatile video utilization. Stages like YouTube, TikTok, and Instagram have engaged people to become content makers and offer their gifts, bits of knowledge, and innovativeness with a worldwide crowd. This democratization of content creation has changed how we draw in with media and amusement.

On YouTube, for example, clients can track down a huge range of content, from instructive instructional exercises and video blogs to gaming transfers and cooking shows. The stage gives a space to makers to articulate their thoughts, construct individual brands, and interface with similar watchers. Content makers frequently have devoted followings, making a feeling of local area and shared enthusiasm around unambiguous interests.

The ascent of powerhouse promoting is one more imperative part of client created content. Powerhouses, people with a significant and drew in web based following, have become pursued brand representatives. Organizations and brands team up with powerhouses to arrive at their main interest group through valid and appealing channels. The powerhouse promoting industry has developed considerably, offering new work open doors for both forces to be reckoned with and advertisers.

Short-structure video stages, like TikTok, have added to the flood of client produced content. These stages have a low boundary to section, permitting anybody with a cell phone and an imaginative plan to turn into a substance maker. The straightforwardness of content creation and the potential for recordings to turn into a web sensation have made short-structure video a profoundly open and engaging mode for computerized articulation.

UGC isn't restricted to amusement; it stretches out to instructive substance too. Instructive YouTubers, frequently alluded to as "Edu-Tubers," have acquired fame by giving connecting with and enlightening recordings on many subjects. Their capacity to separate complex points, make sense of them outwardly, and offer learning assets has made them significant resources in the advanced training scene.

The appeal of client produced content lies in its genuineness and the unique interaction it makes with watchers. Crowds value content that mirrors the genuine encounters and interests of makers. This association can prompt elevated degrees of commitment, trust, and reliability among adherents.

Difficulties and Open doors

While portable video utilization patterns offer various advantages, they additionally present difficulties and open doors for content makers, organizations, and clients the same.

1. **Adaptation and Income Streams**

   One test for content makers is the adaptation of their substance. Stages like YouTube offer income sharing open doors through promotions, yet the pay can be erratic and depends on factors like promotion income rates and watcher commitment. Content makers frequently investigate elective income streams, like brand associations, stock deals, and crowdfunding, to support their inventive undertakings.

   Organizations, then again, consider versatile video utilization to be a chance to interface with a more extensive crowd. The test is in making convincing video content that resounds with clients and converts sees into deals. Promoters need to adjust to the changing media scene, where customers expect pertinent and drawing in happy as opposed to nosy commercials.

2. **Content Discoverability and Algorithmic Curation**

   For both substance makers and organizations, the discoverability of content is pivotal. Calculations on stages like YouTube and web-based entertainment figure out what content is displayed to clients, making it trying to hang out in a jam-packed computerized space. Makers should comprehend and work inside the algorithmic standards of the stages to really arrive at their ideal interest group.

3. **Protection and Information Security**

The ascent of portable video utilization has raised worries about protection and information security. Clients are sharing an abundance of individual data on these stages, and it's fundamental that their information is taken care of safely and dependably. Ongoing information breaks and security embarrassments have featured the requirement for further developed information insurance measures and client command over their data.

4. **Advanced Prosperity and Screen Time***

Over the top screen time, frequently credited to portable video utilization, can unfavorably affect physical and emotional wellness. Issues like computerized eye strain, disturbed rest designs, and a stationary way of life have been connected to unnecessary screen time. Content makers, organizations, and stages need to consider the potential wellbeing effects of their items and content.

5. **Falsehood and Advanced Literacy***

The spread of falsehood and disinformation through portable video content is a developing concern. Video content can be controlled or taken inappropriately, prompting the spread of bogus data. Guaranteeing media proficiency and decisive reasoning abilities are created and kept up with is pivotal for clients to observe dependable sources from temperamental ones.

6. **Rivalry and Quality***

The rising fame of versatile video utilization has prompted a flood in satisfied makers and organizations competing for clients' focus. The test lies in making content that isn't just captivating yet in addition of top caliber. Clients have become knowing and expect proficient creation values, even from novice makers.

| 58 |

4

Chapter 4

Social Interaction and Community

In a world that is progressively associated through computerized innovation, social communication and local area have taken on new aspects. These parts of human existence, which have for quite some time been basic to our reality, have advanced in light of the computerized age. This investigation dives into the diverse idea of social association and local area in the contemporary time, looking at how innovation has both changed and re-imagined the manner in which we interface with each other and structure networks, from the computerized spaces of virtual entertainment to this present reality ramifications of these changes.

The Advanced Transformation and Its Effect on Friendly Connection

The computerized upset, set apart by the broad reception of the web, cell phones, and online entertainment stages, has reshaped the scene of social association. It has democratized correspondence, empowering individuals from all edges of the globe to associate, share, and team up in manners beforehand unbelievable.

1. **The Ascent of Virtual Entertainment**
   Web-based entertainment stages, like Facebook, Twitter, Instagram, and LinkedIn, play had an essential impact in this change. They have become focal centers for online social communication, permitting clients to share individual updates, associate with loved ones, and participate in broad daylight talk. These stages work with relational correspondence as well as the arrangement of advanced networks worked around shared interests, philosophies, and encounters.
   The charm of web-based entertainment lies in its capacity to give a virtual space where clients can articulate their thoughts, keep up with connections, and access data. It permits individuals to remain associated with far off loved ones, spanning geological partitions. Besides, online entertainment stages have become fundamental apparatuses for news scattering, activism, and political commitment, altogether molding public talk and social developments.

2. **The Effect on Private Connections**
   The manner in which we sustain individual connections has additionally been essentially impacted by computerized innovation. Text informing, voice and video calls, and virtual entertainment have extended the opportunities for keeping in contact with friends and family. Remote relationships, which were once supported basically through composed letters and infrequent calls, can now flourish through normal advanced correspondence.
   Computerized innovation has carried the two open doors and difficulties to individual connections. On one hand, it has made it more straightforward for individuals to interface and express friendship, paying little heed to actual distance. Then again, it has raised worries about the nature of advanced cooperations contrasted with face to face correspondence. The computerized domain misses the mark on subtleties of non-verbal communication

and tone, possibly prompting false impressions or misinterpretations.

3. **Web based Dating and Heartfelt Associations**

The advanced age has changed the domain of heartfelt connections through the multiplication of web based dating stages. These applications and sites permit people to associate with potential accomplices in view of shared interests, values, and inclinations. The accommodation and availability of web based dating have prompted critical changes in how individuals look for and lay out heartfelt associations.

While internet dating offers a more extensive pool of possible accomplices, it has likewise brought up issues about the commodification of connections and the effect of innovation on the elements of romance. The computerized climate presents new difficulties, for example, exploring the universe of advanced personas and going up against issues connected with security and wellbeing.

The Development of Local area in the Computerized Age

As friendly cooperation has developed in the advanced age, so too has the idea of local area. Networks, customarily established in geographic nearness or shared actual spaces, have ventured into the advanced domain. Online people group are conformed to normal interests, leisure activities, characters, and causes, setting out exceptional open doors for association and having a place.

1. **Specialty People group and Character**
   Quite possibly of the most prominent advancement in the computerized age is the ascent of specialty networks. There people with quite certain interests, like a specific side interest, being a fan, or way of life, can interface with similar individuals. These people group give a road to individuals to communicate their personalities and find acknowledgment among the people who share their interests.
   Specialty people group have been especially enabling for

underestimated or underrepresented gatherings. Online stages have permitted LGBTQ+ people, individuals with uncommon ailments, and numerous others to find backing and local area in a manner that was not as promptly open in actual spaces. These people group have frequently filled in as places of refuge for people who might not have felt perceived or acknowledged in their nearby actual conditions.

2. **The Impact of Social Developments and Activism**

The computerized age has seen the enhancement of social developments and activism through web-based networks. Online entertainment stages, specifically, have become incredible assets for coordinating, activating, and bringing issues to light about friendly and policy driven issues. Developments like #BlackLives-Matter, #MeToo, and environment activism have outfit the span of advanced stages to impact change and backer for equity.

Online people group assume a focal part in these developments, as they give spaces to individuals to share data, stories, and assets. They encourage a feeling of solidarity and mutual perspective among activists, in any event, when they are topographically scattered. The force of online networks in driving social change features the groundbreaking capability of computerized innovation.

3. **Difficulties of Online People group**

While online networks offer various benefits, they are not without challenges. The computerized climate can some of the time encourage harmful way of behaving, including cyberbullying, badgering, and the spread of can't stand discourse. The general namelessness of online spaces can encourage people to take part in hurtful activities that they probably won't seek after, in actuality.

Moreover, the peculiarity of "protected, closed off environments" has turned into a worry. Online stages will generally suggest content and associations in light of clients' current inclinations and ways of behaving, which can prompt the support of existing convictions and an absence of openness to different perspectives. This can add to polarization and an absence of valuable exchange inside internet based networks.

The Crossing point of Advanced and Actual People group

It's critical to perceive that computerized networks don't exist in detachment. They converge with actual networks and have genuine ramifications. The connections framed in web-based spaces can prompt disconnected communications, for example, meetups, gatherings, and cooperative undertakings. The computerized and actual domains are progressively entwined, obscuring the lines between them.

1. **Geolocation and True Connection**

   The combination of geolocation innovation into cell phones has empowered the assembly of advanced and actual networks. Geolocation administrations permit clients to share their ongoing areas and find close by occasions, organizations, and exercises. This capacity has worked with certifiable cooperations among people who might have at first associated on the web.

   Person to person communication stages, as Facebook and Foursquare, have coordinated geolocation includes that empower clients to check in at explicit areas and offer their whereabouts with companions and adherents. This has prompted the association of unconstrained meetups and get-togethers, as well as the disclosure of neighborhood occasions and organizations.

2. **Publicly supporting and Cooperative Undertakings**

   Advanced people group frequently participate in cooperative undertakings that have genuine effects. Publicly supporting, the act of getting info, thoughts, or content from an enormous gathering, is a prominent model. Online people group can meet up to tackle issues, gather pledges for purposes, or add to explore drives.

   Wikipedia, for example, is a universally cooperative web-based reference book made and kept up with by volunteers. It fills in as a model for the aggregate age of information and data.

Publicly supporting has likewise been utilized in logical exploration, calamity reaction, and local area advancement, showing the potential for computerized networks to make unmistakable, genuine change.

3. The "Meetup" Culture

The "meetup" culture, portrayed by the association of in-person social occasions started on the web, has turned into a characterizing component of the crossing point among computerized and actual networks. Online stages, as Meetup.com, have made it simple for people to make and join bunches based on normal interests or exercises. Individuals from these gatherings can then design and go to physical meetups, going from climbing trips and book clubs to coding studios and expert systems administration occasions.

The meetup culture mirrors the craving for veritable, eye to eye associations in an undeniably advanced world. It permits individuals to consolidate their advanced advantages and online communications with certifiable encounters.

Challenges and Moral Contemplations

As the limits among advanced and actual networks obscure, a few difficulties and moral contemplations arise:

1. **Protection and Information Security**
   The coordination of geolocation innovation raises worries about protection and information security. Clients may unexpectedly unveil touchy data about their whereabouts, possibly endangering their security. The capable utilization of area sharing highlights and severe protection controls are fundamental to moderate these worries.

2. **Advanced Education and Online Way of behaving**
   Computerized people group face the test of advancing computerized education and mindful internet based conduct. Teaching clients about internet based behavior, reality checking, and decisive

reasoning is urgent to establish better web-based conditions and battle deception.

3. **Inclusivity and Openness**

Guaranteeing that computerized networks are comprehensive and open to a different scope of people is a continuous test. Hindrances connected with innovation access, advanced abilities, and online provocation can keep certain individuals from completely partaking in or profiting from these networks.

4. **Information Possession and Control**

The topic of information possession and control is a critical moral thought. Clients frequently share individual data and content on advanced stages, bringing up issues about who claims this information, the way things are utilized, and what freedoms people have over their computerized commitments.

5. **Moral Obligation**

The impact and effect of advanced networks on society require a moral obligation with respect to stage administrators and local area pioneers. These partners should consider the expected outcomes of their foundation and address issues connected with control, content arrangements, and client wellbeing.

The computerized age has reclassified the idea of social collaboration and local area. The approach of virtual entertainment, internet dating, and specialty networks has extended the opportunities for interfacing with others and framing significant connections. Computerized stages have likewise assumed a vital part in enhancing social developments and bringing issues to light about basic issues.

The crossing point of computerized and actual networks has set out open doors for certifiable cooperations and cooperative tasks. Geolocation innovation, the meetup culture, and publicly supporting drives represent the potential for advanced networks to have unmistakable, true effects.

Be that as it may, these headways are not without challenges and moral contemplations. Issues connected with security, advanced proficiency, inclusivity, information proprietorship, and moral obligation should be tended to as we explore this developing computerized scene.

Eventually, the computerized age has introduced another period of social collaboration and local area, one that is described by both the uncommon open doors for association and the requirement for capable and moral commitment. As innovation keeps on developing, so too will how we might interpret how computerized and actual networks converge and shape the manner in which we interface with each other.

4.1 The influence of video apps on social connections.

The ascent of video applications has in a general sense changed the scene of social associations in the computerized age. These applications, like Zoom, Skype, FaceTime, and all the more as of late, TikTok and Snapchat, have empowered people to convey, make, and offer video satisfied effortlessly and openness. This investigation digs into the complex impact of video applications on friendly associations, inspecting their effect on private connections, proficient communications, diversion, and self-articulation.

The Development of Video Applications

Video applications have progressed significantly since the beginning of video conferencing, which was basically utilized for business purposes. The appearance of fast web and the omnipresence of cell phones have made it feasible for video correspondence to arrive at the majority. Today, video applications have developed into flexible instruments that serve different capabilities and take special care of assorted crowds.

1. **Individual Correspondence and Connections**

   The impact of video applications on private correspondence is maybe the most striking. Video calls have turned into an essential method of remaining associated with friends and family, especially when actual distance isolates individuals. The capacity to see and hear loved ones continuously overcomes any barrier between eye to eye collaborations and advanced correspondence. Video calls offer a degree of profound association that instant messages and voice calls alone can't repeat. They empower clients to notice looks, motions, and non-verbal communication, which are significant components of human correspondence. For the overwhelming majority, video calls have turned into a life saver during occasions that forestall actual social events, like the Coronavirus pandemic.

2. **Remote Relationships**

Video applications have upset the elements of far-removed relationships. Couples, companions, and families isolated by geology can keep a feeling of fellowship through video calls. The capacity to share encounters, for example, commending birthday celebrations, going to unique events, or just having an easygoing discussion, is priceless in supporting close to home associations.

These applications have likewise become fundamental for military families, worldwide connections, and individuals with friends and family in helped living offices. The comfort and availability of video calls mitigate the aggravation of actual division and proposition snapshots of real association.

3. **The Impact of Video Applications on Sentiment**

Video applications have fundamentally influenced the domain of sentiment and dating. Web based dating stages, similar to Kindling and Blunder, presently consolidate video includes that permit clients to associate through video assembles before conference face to face. This component empowers people to check science, realness, and similarity in a more intelligent and nuanced way.

The Coronavirus pandemic sped up the reception of video dating, with many singles going to video applications as a protected and helpful method for interfacing during lockdowns and social separating measures. While starting distrust encompassed virtual dating, video applications have shown to be powerful in encouraging associations and giving a stage to significant discussions.

4. **Proficient and Instructive Applications**

Video applications have additionally reshaped proficient and instructive communications. Video conferencing stages, like Zoom and Microsoft Groups, have become basic to remote work, internet learning, and virtual coordinated effort. The capacity to lead gatherings, talks, and meetings through video applications has in a general sense changed the manner in which we work and learn. Video conferencing has worked with worldwide coordinated effort, empowering experts and understudies to associate with companions, tutors, and specialists around the world. It has given open doors to remote work, working from home, and online training, giving people more prominent adaptability and admittance to a more extensive scope of assets.

5. **Diversion and Content Creation**

Media outlets has seen a flood in the impact of video applications. Stages like TikTok and Snapchat have upset the manner in which we make, share, and consume video content. These applications engage clients to put themselves out there, recount stories, and engage crowds through short, captivating video cuts.

TikTok, specifically, has turned into a social peculiarity, permitting clients to take part in viral difficulties, grandstand their gifts, and earn respect for their imagination. The application's algorithmic substance disclosure highlight has pushed obscure people to web fame, showing the democratizing force of video applications. Snapchat, then again, presented the idea of "vanishing" or vaporous substance. Clients can share photographs and recordings that evaporate before long, giving a novel and more confidential type of self-articulation. This element has changed how individuals impart and associate through visual substance.

6. **The Effect on Self-Articulation**

Video applications have given a stage to self-articulation and innovativeness that stretches out past media outlets. Clients can catch snapshots of their lives, archive encounters, and offer their considerations through video content. This type of self-articulation has turned into a focal piece of computerized character and the manner in which we introduce ourselves on the web.

TikTok, for example, urges clients to make content that mirrors their characters, interests, and encounters. It has brought forth a culture of genuine, interesting, and various substance that reverberates with an expansive crowd. The impact of video applications on self-articulation has additionally brought about happy makers, vloggers, and powerhouses who utilize the medium to interface with their adherents and offer their viewpoints.

The Effect on Friendly Cooperations

The impact of video applications stretches out past private connections and content creation. It significantly affects social cooperations, encouraging a feeling of network, refinement, and credibility in computerized correspondence.

1. **Refining Advanced Associations**

   Video applications have refined computerized cooperations by giving a more profound degree of association. While text and voice correspondence offer comfort, video calls add a layer of closeness and realness that causes computerized trades to feel more private and certified. The capacity to see looks and non-verbal prompts upgrades the nature of correspondence.

2. **Cultivating Compassion and Understanding**

   Video applications have worked with sympathy and figuring out in web-based communications. They permit clients to observe and value the feelings and encounters of others, making it simpler to connect with their sentiments and viewpoints. Video calls can possibly determine false impressions more really than text or voice correspondence.

3. Diminishing Sensations of Segregation

Video applications have been instrumental in diminishing sensations of disconnection, especially during seasons of social removing and actual partition. For people who might not be able to meet in that frame of mind to geological limitations or well-being concerns, video calls offer a life saver to keep up with social associations and ease dejection.

4. Fighting Computerized Weariness

The impact of video applications on friendly connections has likewise added to battling advanced weariness. While innovation can possibly be overpowering, video applications offer a more adjusted way to deal with computerized correspondence. They add a human touch to online connections, diminishing the feeling of screen-interceded disengagement.

Challenges and Moral Contemplations

The inescapable reception of video applications has achieved difficulties and moral contemplations that warrant consideration.

1. Protection and Security

Protection and security are critical worries while utilizing video applications. Clients might be defenseless against information breaks, unapproved access, and likely abuse of video content. Guaranteeing the security of video correspondence is fundamentally important for people and associations.

2. Computerized Behavior

As video calls become more common in both individual and expert settings, the requirement for computerized manners and gracious way of behaving has become obvious. Clients should know about the fitting standards for video correspondence, including dressing expertly, keeping in touch, and limiting interruptions.

3. Close to home Cost

Video applications have raised worries about the close to home cost of steady virtual correspondence. The sensation of being "on camera" and the consistent perceivability can prompt advanced weakness, stress, and profound depletion. Clients ought to be aware of the effect of video approaches their prosperity and look for balance in their computerized associations.

4. **Inclusivity and Openness**

Video applications, while profoundly useful, may not be available to all people. Individuals with handicaps or restricted admittance to innovation might confront difficulties in partaking in video correspondence. Guaranteeing inclusivity and obliging assorted needs is a moral thought for the people who plan and use video applications.

Video applications have affected social associations in the computerized age. They have changed individual correspondence, proficient communications, diversion, and self-articulation. The impact of video applications stretches out past comfort; it envelops the adaptation of advanced cooperations, encouraging sympathy and grasping, lessening sensations of disengagement, and battling computerized weariness.

While the effect of video applications is predominantly sure, it is fundamental for address the difficulties and moral contemplations related with their utilization. Protection and security, computerized decorum, the close to home cost, inclusivity, and availability are fundamental angles that request consideration.

As video applications proceed to develop and shape the manner in which we associate with others, it is critical to figure out some kind of harmony between the comfort and realness they offer while being aware of their moral ramifications. The impact of video applications on friendly associations isn't simply a mechanical pattern; it addresses an extraordinary change in the manner in which we impart and communicate with each other in the computerized age.

4.2 User engagement and interaction on platforms like TikTok and Instagram.

The computerized age has achieved a transformation in the manner individuals draw in and collaborate with each other, because of online entertainment stages like TikTok and Instagram. These stages have in a general sense changed the scene of client commitment and collaboration, giving a space to self-articulation, imagination, and local area building. In this investigation, we will dig into the multi-layered universe of client commitment and collaboration on TikTok and Instagram, analyzing how these stages have reshaped the manner in which we associate with content, makers, and networks.

The Ascent of TikTok and Instagram

TikTok and Instagram have quickly ascended to noticeable quality in the online entertainment scene, each offering a special arrangement of highlights that take care of many clients.

1. **TikTok**

   TikTok, sent off in 2016, is a short-structure video stage that permits clients to make, share, and find brief video cuts set up with a good soundtrack or other sound. It immediately acquired ubiquity among more youthful socioeconomics for its easy to use interface, engaging substance, and the capacity to turn into a web sensation with only a couple of moments of spellbinding video.

2. **Instagram**

Instagram, at first sent off in 2010 as a photograph sharing stage, has developed into a flexible application that envelops photographs, recordings, Stories, Reels, IGTV, and the sky is the limit from there. Instagram has turned into a visual-driven stage with an accentuation on narrating through sight and sound substance. With more than a billion dynamic clients, it has arisen as a diverse center for individual articulation and computerized association.

Client Commitment on TikTok

Client commitment on TikTok is portrayed by the fast and vivid nature of the stage, driven by a few key elements:

1. **Algorithmic Substance Revelation**

   TikTok's suggestion calculation is vital to its client commitment. The stage utilizes AI to dissect client conduct and inclinations, conveying an organized feed of content custom fitted to every client. This implies that clients are continually presented to recordings that line up with their inclinations, bringing about longer and more regular utilization.

2. **Scroll-First Point of interaction**

   TikTok's point of interaction supports a "scroll-first" approach, where clients can easily swipe up to move starting with one video then onto the next. This plan advances fast utilization and urges clients to burn through broadened periods on the application. The auto-play include guarantees that content continues streaming, keeping up with client commitment.

3. **Client Created Difficulties and Patterns**

   TikTok flourishes with client produced moves and patterns that welcome clients to partake and make their own adaptations. These patterns urge clients to draw in with content, recreate famous difficulties, and put their one of a kind twist on them. The cutthroat and intelligent nature of these patterns is a vital driver of client commitment.

4. **Intelligence and Commitment Highlights**

TikTok offers a scope of intuitive elements that improve client commitment, like two part harmonies, join, remarks, and likes. These elements empower clients to connect straightforwardly with content and makers, encouraging a feeling of local area and collaboration. The capacity to fasten together video reactions or two part harmony with different clients is an unmistakable type of commitment interesting to TikTok.

Client Association on Instagram

Client connection on Instagram is complex and is portrayed by the accompanying key components:

1. **Visual Narrating**

   Instagram is known for its accentuation on visual narrating. Clients can share photographs and recordings that convey their encounters, yearnings, and day to day existence. This visual part of the stage has made a feeling of association through shared minutes and style.

2. **The Force of Hashtags**

   Hashtags on Instagram act as an incredible asset for content revelation and collaboration. Clients can investigate content connected with explicit hashtags, find new records, and draw in with a more extensive local area keen on similar themes. Hashtags energize discussions and client created patterns, like TikTok.

3. **Stories and Live Streams**

   Instagram's Accounts highlight and live streaming capacities give continuous connection and genuineness. Clients can draw in with their devotees through Stories, offering looks into their everyday lives, or go live to associate with a crowd of people straightforwardly. Live back and forth discussions, in the background looks, and intuitive difficulties are well known types of cooperation through Stories and live streams.

4. **Direct Informing**

   Instagram's immediate informing highlight empowers private discussions and connections between clients. It is frequently utilized for one-on-one correspondence, sharing substance, and building further associations. Instagram's joining with Facebook Courier has extended informing abilities.

5. **Client Produced Content**

Client produced content (UGC) assumes a huge part in Instagram's biological system. UGC includes clients making content connected with a brand or a particular subject, frequently using a marked hashtag. This type of association empowers interest and commitment with brands and networks.

Powerhouse Culture and Client Commitment

Both TikTok and Instagram have added to the ascent of powerhouse culture, where content makers, frequently with enormous followings, team up with brands and draw in with their crowds. Forces to be reckoned with assume a huge part in forming client commitment on these stages.

1. **TikTok Forces to be reckoned with**

   TikTok has led to another age of powerhouses who make viral substance, take part in patterns, and draw in with their adherents. These powerhouses frequently fabricate a profoundly drawn in and faithful fan base. Brands cooperate with TikTok powerhouses to arrive at more youthful socioeconomics and influence their innovative substance for advertising.

2. **Instagram Powerhouses**

Instagram has for some time been a stage where powerhouses have flourished. Instagram forces to be reckoned with come in different specialties, including style, way of life, travel, wellness, and then some. They draw in with their devotees through organized content, coordinated efforts, supported posts, and stories. Instagram forces to be reckoned with have the ability to shape drifts and acquaint their crowds with new items and encounters.

Client Created Patterns and Difficulties

The two stages have seen the production of client created patterns and difficulties that fundamentally influence client commitment.

1. **TikTok Patterns and Difficulties**

   TikTok difficulties and patterns frequently start with a solitary video or idea and immediately pick up speed as clients take an interest and add their exceptional turns. These patterns are a main thrust behind the stage's steady stream of drawing in satisfied. Models incorporate dance difficulties, lip-sync patterns, and cooking hacks.

2. **Instagram Difficulties and Hashtags**

Instagram challenges and hashtags have turned into a way for clients to draw in with more extensive networks and exhibit their imagination. Difficulties could include posting a themed photograph, taking part in a particular action, or offering content to a specific hashtag. These difficulties support client communication and interest.

Building People group and Fandoms

Both TikTok and Instagram empower clients to assemble and take part in networks and fandoms, frequently revolved around shared interests, leisure activities, or fanbases.

1. **TikTok People group**

   TikTok people group structure around unambiguous substance specialties and interests. Clients make and consume content connected with their interests, associating with other people who share similar interests. The remark areas of recordings become spaces for collaboration and conversation inside these networks.

2. **Instagram Fandoms**

Instagram is a stage where fandoms for famous people, powerhouses, and brands flourish. Clients follow, draw in with, and commend the substance and accomplishments of their #1 figures. Instagram cultivates a feeling of having a place and association among fans.

Challenges and Moral Contemplations

The unique universe of client commitment and connection on TikTok and Instagram likewise presents difficulties and moral contemplations:

1. **Protection and Information**

   Protection and information security are huge worries on the

two stages. Clients share individual data and content, frequently without completely grasping the ramifications. Guaranteeing the assurance of client information is really difficult for stage administrators.

2. **Emotional well-being**

The consistent openness to organized content and the strain to keep a glorified internet based persona can adversely affect psychological well-being. Clients might encounter insecurities, correlation, and social uneasiness. The quest for preferences and approval can prompt unfortunate commitment designs.

3. **Cyberbullying and Badgering**

The two stages are helpless to cyberbullying and provocation. Savages and malevolent clients can target people with terrible remarks or unsafe way of behaving. Combatting on the web misuse and badgering is a common obligation of clients, stage administrators, and networks.

4. **Enslavement and Computerized Prosperity**

The exceptionally captivating nature of TikTok and Instagram can prompt habit-forming utilization designs. Consistent looking over and the feeling of dread toward passing up a great opportunity (FOMO) can negatively affect clients' prosperity. Advancing computerized proficiency, care, and dependable utilization is fundamental.

5. **Inclusivity and Portrayal**

The stages need to resolve issues of inclusivity and portrayal. Guaranteeing different voices and points of view are heard and addressed is critical for cultivating a more comprehensive and impartial internet based climate.

Chapter 5

From Consumers to Creators

The computerized age has seen a significant change in the job of people in the web-based scene. Never again are individuals latent purchasers of content; they have become dynamic makers, molding the advanced world through client created content (UGC). This change has in a general sense modified the elements of data, diversion, and culture. In this investigation, we dig into the development of client created content, looking at how it has enabled people, reshaped ventures, and reclassified the idea of origin.

The Beginning of Client Created Content

The idea of client produced content arose with the approach of the web and the democratization of data sharing. In the beginning of the Internet, people started to distribute their contemplations, encounters, and imaginative chips away at individual sites, discussions, and online journals. This obvious the start of a shift from detached utilization to dynamic cooperation in computerized content creation.

1. Individual Websites and Discussions

Individual online journals and gatherings gave early stages to clients to share their contemplations and encounters. These spaces permitted people to lay out their web-based presence and associate with similar individuals. The substance went from individual journals and travel logs to specialty leisure activity discussions, showing the variety of client interests.

2. **Web 2.0 and the Online Entertainment Unrest**
   The change to Web 2.0 presented another period of client created satisfied with the ascent of virtual entertainment stages. These stages, like MySpace, Facebook, and YouTube, empowered clients to share message, photographs, recordings, and connections. The simplicity of content creation and sharing changed how individuals interfaced with computerized media.

3. **YouTube and the Introduction of Video Content Makers**

YouTube, sent off in 2005, assumed a urgent part in the development of client created content, especially in the domain of video. It gave a space to people to transfer, share, and find recordings on many points. This democratization of video creation established the groundwork for the rise of content makers and powerhouses.

The Strengthening of Client Created Content

Client created content has enabled people in more ways than one:

1. **Self-Articulation and Inventiveness**
   Client produced content offers a method for self-articulation and inventiveness. Clients can share their interests, interests, and gifts with a worldwide crowd. The demonstration of creation turns into a source for individual articulation, and the computerized world gives a material to different types of content, from composed articles and photography to music and video.

2. **Local area Building**
   Client created content encourages local area building and associations among similar people. Online people group structure around shared interests, leisure activities, and causes. Clients

associate with each other, offer help, and take part in conversations. The web turns into a center point for specialty networks and subcultures that might not have flourished in any case.

3. **Individual Marking**

Client created content has empowered individual marking, permitting people to set up a good foundation for themselves as specialists, specialists, or powerhouses in their separate fields. Content makers assemble individual brands that mirror their personality and ability, drawing in adherents who esteem their substance and viewpoints.

4. **Business and Pay Age**

Client created content has opened entryways for business venture and pay age. Content makers can adapt their work through publicizing, supported content, stock, and crowdfunding. Stages like YouTube and Patreon offer makers the valuable chance to transform their interests into an economical vocation.

The Ascent of Virtual Entertainment Forces to be reckoned with

The ascent of virtual entertainment forces to be reckoned with addresses a huge development of client produced content. Forces to be reckoned with are people who have amassed a significant following on stages like Instagram, TikTok, and Twitter. They take advantage of their leverage to advance items, causes, and thoughts. The force to be reckoned with peculiarity has re-imagined the elements of showcasing and brand supports.

1. **Miniature Forces to be reckoned with**

Miniature powerhouses are people with a more modest yet exceptionally drew in following. They are in many cases more appealing to their crowd and are viewed as specialists in specialty fields. Marks progressively team up with miniature powerhouses to arrive at explicit socioeconomics and networks.

2. **Credibility and Trust**

   Powerhouses are esteemed for their legitimacy and the trust they work with their supporters. They frequently share individual stories, encounters, and sincere bits of knowledge, which resound with their crowd. This legitimacy recognizes them from customary VIPs.

3. **Molding Customer Conduct**

Forces to be reckoned with significantly affect purchaser conduct. Their suggestions and supports can impact buying choices. Brands perceive the force of powerhouse showcasing in coming to and drawing in with their interest groups.

The Extraordinary Force of Publicly supporting

Publicly supporting is one more indication of client created content, where an aggregate gathering of people adds to an undertaking, drive, or thought. This approach has been extraordinary in different areas:

1. **Resident News-casting**

   Publicly supporting plays had a critical impact in resident news-casting. Regular people utilize their cell phones to catch and share news occasions, adding to a more extensive comprehension of worldwide occasions. Stages like Twitter have become center points for constant announcing and observer accounts.

2. **Open-Source Programming**

   Open-source programming depends on commitments from a worldwide local area of engineers. This cooperative methodology has brought about generally utilized programming and stages, for example, the Linux working framework, WordPress, and the Mozilla Firefox internet browser.

3. **Crowdfunding**

   Crowdfunding stages like Kickstarter and Indiegogo permit people to subsidize imaginative tasks and enterprising endeavors.

Benefactors play an immediate part in rejuvenating thoughts, from creative items to narrative movies.

4. Critical thinking and Advancement

Publicly supporting has turned into an incredible asset for critical thinking and development. Organizations and associations tap into the aggregate insight of the group to track down arrangements, decide, and drive progress.

Challenges and Moral Contemplations

The development of client produced content likewise raises difficulties and moral contemplations:

1. **Deception and Disinformation**

   Client produced content can add to the spread of deception and disinformation. Bogus or misdirecting data can build up some decent momentum and contact a wide crowd. Stages and clients should be cautious in confirming and truth really taking a look at content.

2. **Protection and Information Security**

   The assortment and sharing of individual data through client created content raise worries about protection and information security. Clients ought to know about the data they share on the web and the expected outcomes.

3. **Copyright and Protected innovation**

   Issues connected with copyright and licensed innovation are critical with regards to client produced content. Content makers and stages should explore the intricacies of intellectual property regulation, fair use, and protected innovation freedoms.

4. **Emotional well-being and Prosperity**

   The quest for preferences, remarks, and social approval in the domain of client created content can adversely affect emotional wellness. Clients might encounter serious insecurities, correlation, and social nervousness. Stages should consider the prosperity of their clients.

5. The Spread of Disdain Discourse and Unsafe Substance

Client produced content stages are not resistant to the spread of disdain discourse, provocation, and hurtful substance. Guaranteeing client security and tending to oppressive way of behaving are basic responsibilities regarding stage administrators.

5.1 The power of user-generated content.

Client produced content (UGC) has arisen as a strong and extraordinary power in the computerized age. It incorporates an extensive variety of content made by people as opposed to conventional news sources or companies. From web-based entertainment posts, item surveys, sites, video blogs, and web recordings to photographs, recordings, and social remarks, UGC has turned into a vital piece of the web-based insight. In this investigation, we will dig into the significant effect and meaning of client produced content, looking at how it has reshaped businesses, impacted buyer conduct, and engaged people to become makers and powerhouses by their own doing.

The Pervasiveness of Client Created Content

Client created content is wherever in the present advanced scene. It pervades virtually every edge of the web and incorporates different types of articulation and commitment. Web-based entertainment stages like Facebook, Instagram, and Twitter are overflowing with UGC, as are devoted substance sharing stages like YouTube, TikTok, and Medium. Coming up next are a few vital indications of client produced content:

1. **Online Entertainment Posts and Remarks**
   Clients consistently share their contemplations, encounters, and sentiments via virtual entertainment stages. Whether it's posting refreshes about their lives, remarking on recent developments, or taking part in conversations, these stages act as a center for client produced content.

2. **Item Surveys and Appraisals**

   Web based business sites, like Amazon and Howl, are overflowing with client created item audits and evaluations. Potential purchasers frequently depend on the encounters and assessments of individual shoppers while settling on buying choices.

3. **Online journals and Individual Sites**

   Web journals and individual sites have engaged people to make and share composed content on a large number of points. Bloggers and content makers frequently become experts in their specialties, drawing in committed crowds.

4. **Video Sharing**

   Video stages like YouTube, TikTok, and Vimeo have empowered clients to make, transfer, and offer video content. The ascent of video makers and powerhouses has changed the manner in which individuals consume diversion and data.

5. **Photography and Visual Substance**

Photograph sharing stages like Instagram and Flickr have brought about photography devotees who exhibit their work and move others. Visual substance has turned into a prevailing type of correspondence and articulation.

The Effect on Enterprises and Organizations

The impact of client produced content reaches out a long ways past individual articulation. It has essentially reshaped ventures and disturbed customary models in different ways.

1. **Media outlets**

   Client created content has tested the conventional media outlet. YouTube makers, for instance, have amassed huge number of supporters and produce significant pay through promoting and associations. Client produced content has additionally led to internet real time stages, where people make and offer unique shows and series.

2. **News-casting and News Announcing**

   Client produced content significantly affects reporting. Resident columnists and onlookers use cell phones to catch and share news situation as they transpire. Online entertainment stages assume a focal part in dispersing continuous news and giving a different scope of points of view.

3. **Promoting and Publicizing**

   Organizations have perceived the worth of client produced content in showcasing and promoting. Customers frequently trust peer surveys and suggestions more than customary publicizing. Brands have bridled the force of client created content by empowering clients to share their encounters and collaborate with marked content.

4. **Travel and The travel industry**

   The movement business has been changed by client produced content. Voyagers share their encounters, suggestions, and photographs on stages like TripAdvisor and Instagram, impacting others' movement choices. Travel bloggers and vloggers have become persuasive figures in the business.

5. **Item Improvement**

Organizations influence client created content to illuminate item improvement. Client audits and input can prompt item upgrades, improved elements, and better client encounters.

The Impact on Buyer Conduct

Client produced content assumes a urgent part in molding customer conduct and direction. A few key variables add to its impact:

1. **Legitimacy and Trust**

   Customers frequently trust client created content more than conventional publicizing. Audits, tributes, and firsthand records feel genuine and engaging. Credibility is a sign of UGC, and this straightforwardness encourages trust.

2. **Social Confirmation**

   Social confirmation, the mental peculiarity where individuals follow the activities of others, is a strong power in purchaser conduct. At the point when people see that others have had positive encounters with an item or administration, they are bound to pursue comparative decisions.

3. **Peer Proposals**

   Client produced content frequently fills in as companion proposals. At the point when companions or colleagues share their encounters and supports, it conveys more weight with customers. Informal organizations permit clients to impact their friends' decisions.

4. **Inside and out Data**

   Client created content can give top to bottom data and understanding that might be deficient in customary item depictions or commercials. Purchasers can acquire a more far reaching comprehension of an item or administration through surveys and point by point encounters.

5. **Genuine Models**

Client created content frequently exhibits certifiable models and situations. These down to earth shows assist shoppers with imagining how an item or administration could help them in their day to day routines.

The Ascent of Powerhouses and Content Makers

The peculiarity of forces to be reckoned with and content makers is an immediate consequence of the force of client produced content. These people, frequently with significant followings, influence their impact to shape customer conduct and advance items and administrations.

1. **Content Makers**

   Content makers on stages like YouTube, Instagram, and TikTok produce unique substance that can incorporate item surveys, instructional exercises, and way of life video blogs. These makers construct a dedicated and drew in crowd, frequently founded on their skill, realness, or charm.

2. **Miniature Forces to be reckoned with**

   Miniature powerhouses are people with more modest yet profoundly drew in followings. They frequently represent considerable authority in specialty regions, like wellness, travel, or excellence. Marks progressively team up with miniature powerhouses to target explicit socioeconomics and networks.

3. **Brand Coordinated efforts**

Powerhouses team up with brands to make supported content. These organizations frequently obscure the lines between customary promoting and client produced content. Powerhouses incorporate brand informing consistently into their substance, making it more engaging to their crowd.

The Groundbreaking Force of Publicly supporting

Publicly supporting, a subset of client created content, includes getting thoughts, content, administrations, or commitments by requesting input from an enormous gathering or "group." It has extraordinarily affected different spaces:

1. **Resident Science**

   Resident science projects outfit the force of the group to gather information and direct examination. Volunteers add to logical drives, like following untamed life, observing natural changes, and planning heavenly bodies.

2. **Open-Source Programming**

   Open-source programming depends on the cooperative endeavors of a worldwide local area of engineers. This model has brought about generally utilized programming and stages, including the Linux working framework, WordPress, and the Mozilla Firefox internet browser.

3. **Crowdfunding**

   Crowdfunding stages like Kickstarter and Indiegogo empower people to finance inventive activities and innovative endeavors. Supporters play an immediate part in rejuvenating creative thoughts, from tech new businesses to imaginative undertakings.

4. **Critical thinking and Advancement**

Publicly supporting has turned into a useful asset for critical thinking and development. Organizations and associations tap into the aggregate insight of the group to track down arrangements, decide, and drive progress.

Challenges and Moral Contemplations

While client created content has achieved huge advantages and open doors, it additionally presents difficulties and moral contemplations:

1. **Deception and Disinformation**

   Client produced content can add to the spread of deception and disinformation. Bogus or deceiving data can build up some forward momentum and contact a wide crowd. Guaranteeing precise and solid data is a continuous test.

2. **Protection and Information Security**

   The assortment and sharing of individual data through client produced content raise worries about protection and information security. Clients should know about the data they share on the web and the likely outcomes.

3. **Copyright and Licensed innovation**

   Issues connected with copyright and protected innovation are critical with regards to client created content. Content makers and stages should explore the intricacies of intellectual property regulation, fair use, and licensed innovation privileges.

4. **Emotional wellness and Prosperity**

   The quest for preferences, remarks, and social approval in the domain of client produced content can adversely affect emotional wellness. Clients might encounter deep-seated insecurities, correlation, and social nervousness. Stages should consider the prosperity of their clients.

5. **The Spread of Disdain Discourse and Destructive Substance**

Client produced content stages are not resistant to the spread of disdain discourse, provocation, and destructive substance. Guaranteeing client wellbeing and tending to oppressive way of behaving are basic responsibilities regarding stage administrators.

5.2 How individuals become influencers and creators.

The computerized age has opened up exceptional open doors for people to become powerhouses and makers, molding their own stories and hoarding committed crowds. The ascent of online entertainment, content-sharing stages, and the democratization of data has changed the manner in which we associate, impart, and consume content. In this investigation, we will dive into the excursion of how people become powerhouses and makers, analyzing the means, methodologies, and difficulties engaged with this extraordinary cycle.

The Time of Advanced Strengthening

The computerized age has led to a change in outlook in the manner in which people can use innovation to become forces to be reckoned with and makers. This change is described by a few key components:

1. **Admittance to Innovation**

   Admittance to cell phones, reasonable cameras, and easy to use programming has become boundless, engaging people to deliver great substance. The hindrances to section have been fundamentally brought down, permitting anybody with an inventive vision to take an interest.

2. **Online Stages**

   A huge number of online stages and virtual entertainment networks have arisen, giving a phase to people to exhibit their gifts, share their insight, or interface with similar individuals. From

YouTube and Instagram to TikTok and podcasting stages, these spaces offer the perceivability and arrive at that were once held for conventional news sources.

3. **The Force of Specialty People group**
   Advanced spaces have permitted people to associate with specialty networks and subcultures that share their inclinations and interests. This designated commitment empowers makers to track down their one of a kind crowd and fabricate associations with their devotees.

4. **Adaptation Amazing open doors**

The computerized scene offers different adaptation valuable open doors for powerhouses and makers, from promoting and sponsorships to stock, item supports, and crowdfunding. Makers can transform their enthusiasm into a feasible vocation.

The Excursion to Turning into a Powerhouse or Maker

The way to turning into a powerhouse or maker includes a few vital stages and methodologies:

1. **Distinguishing an Enthusiasm or Specialty**
   The excursion frequently starts enthusiastically or skill in a specific field or specialty. Makers ought to distinguish what genuinely invigorates them and what they can propose to a particular crowd. This could incorporate regions like travel, style, gaming, food, innovation, wellbeing, or even subcultures like retro gaming, vegetarian cooking, or specialty leisure activities.

2. **Making Top notch Content**
   Reliably making excellent substance is central to building a presence as a powerhouse or maker. This content can take different structures, including:
   Composed Content: Blog entries, articles, or digital books.
   Visual Substance: Photographs, representations, and infographics.

Sound Substance: Web recordings and music.

Video Content: YouTube recordings, video blogs, instructional exercises, and movements.

The decision of content configuration ought to line up with the maker's assets and the inclinations of their interest group.

3. **Building an Internet based Presence**

A web-based presence starts with setting up profiles on applicable stages and enhancing them for revelation. This incorporates making drawing in profiles, choosing profile photographs, and giving clear and succinct depictions of what's going on with the maker. Being predictable across stages helps clients perceive and recall the maker.

4. **Consistency and Recurrence**

Consistency and routineness in happy creation are vital to growing a crowd of people. Makers ought to lay out a posting plan that suits their capacities and the assumptions for their crowd. The recurrence of content ought to keep up with crowd commitment and expectation.

5. **Commitment and Local area Building**

Drawing in with the crowd is a basic piece of building a following. Makers ought to answer remarks, seek clarification on pressing issues, and encourage conversations to make a feeling of local area. The more connected with the crowd, the more faithful and strong they become.

6. **Joint efforts and Systems administration**

Joint efforts with different makers and systems administration inside the specialty can assist with growing a maker's span. Joining forces with similar people can acquaint the maker with new crowds and cultivate cross-advancement.

7. **Adaptation Techniques**

Adaptation techniques might include different methodologies:

Publicizing: Cooperating with sponsors or promotion organizations to show advertisements on satisfied.

Sponsorships: Teaming up with brands for supported content or supports.

Stock: Selling marked product or items.

Item Deals: Creating and selling items or administrations.

Member Showcasing: Advancing items or administrations and procuring a commission for every deal created.

Adaptation ought to line up with the maker's qualities and the interests of their crowd.

Difficulties and Contemplations

Turning into a powerhouse or maker isn't without its difficulties and contemplations. Makers ought to know about the accompanying:

1. **Contest**

   The internet based scene is exceptionally serious, with a great many people competing for focus and devotees. Standing apart requires uniqueness, innovativeness, and assurance.

2. **Time and Persistence**

   Building a huge following and accomplishing powerhouse status takes time and tolerance. It's anything but a mind-blowing phenomenon yet rather an excursion that requires commitment and perseverance.

3. **Content Quality**

   Reliably delivering excellent substance can interest. Makers should put resources into their abilities, gear, and information to keep up with and work on the nature of their substance.

4. **Crowd Commitment**

   Drawing in with a group of people can be tedious yet is fundamental for building a reliable following. Makers ought to be ready to consistently cooperate with their crowd.

5. **Transformation and Advancement**

   The computerized scene is steadily developing. Makers should adjust to evolving stages, calculations, and patterns. Development and the capacity to remain important are urgent.

6. Psychological well-being and Prosperity

The quest for powerhouse or maker status can affect emotional well-being and prosperity. Makers might encounter pressure, burnout, and the consistent mission for social approval. Taking care of oneself and keeping a sound balance between serious and fun activities are fundamental.

The Job of Realness

Realness is a foundation of progress for powerhouses and makers. Crowds esteem validity and straightforwardness. Makers who stay consistent with themselves, share their encounters, and interface on an individual level will generally fabricate more significant and enduring associations with their devotees.

Contextual analysis: The YouTube Maker

To represent the excursion of turning into a maker, we should consider the instance of a YouTube content maker.

1. **Distinguishing an Energy or Specialty**

   Our yearning YouTube maker has a profound enthusiasm for cooking, especially trying different things with global recipes. They choose to zero in their channel on sharing their culinary experiences and giving simple to-follow cooking instructional exercises.

2. **Making Great Substance**

   The maker puts resources into a decent camera, mouthpiece, and video altering programming to create great cooking recordings. They focus on lighting, sound quality, and connecting with show.

3. **Building a Web-based Presence**

   The maker makes a YouTube channel, modifies their profile with an essential logo, and composes an instructive "About" segment.

They pick a channel name that mirrors their specialty and their energy for global cooking.

4. **Consistency and Recurrence**

To connect with their crowd reliably, the maker transfers another cooking video consistently. They declare their transfer plan and communicate with watchers through remarks.

5. **Commitment and Local area Building**

The maker effectively answers remarks, addresses cooking-related questions, and urges watchers to share their encounters. They likewise run incidental cooking difficulties to encourage a feeling of local area.

6. **Joint efforts and Systems administration**

The maker teams up with individual food lovers on visitor recordings and cross-advancements. They network inside food-related networks to extend their span.

7. **Adaptation Methodologies**

As the channel develops, the maker investigates adaptation choices. They collaborate with kitchen gear organizations for supported recordings, make a line of cooking-related stock, and incorporate partner connects to cooking tools in video portrayals.

The YouTube maker's process is set apart by their energy for cooking and their obligation to offering some benefit to their crowd. Over the long run, their devotion, realness, and the nature of their substance assist them with building a flourishing channel.

The excursion from being a person to turning into a powerhouse or maker in the computerized age is portrayed by enthusiasm, consistency, commitment, and genuineness. While it presents difficulties and requests devotion, the prizes are significant. People have the valuable chance to share their mastery, fabricate networks, and even transform their enthusiasm into a reasonable profession.

Validness is a focal mainstay of this excursion, as crowds esteem certifiable, engaging, and straightforward substance. Makers who interface on an individual level with their devotees frequently construct further, more significant connections.

The advanced scene proceeds to develop, and new open doors arise routinely. Hopeful forces to be reckoned with and makers ought to remain versatile, embrace advancement, and stay consistent with their interests and values. Eventually, the way to turning into a powerhouse or maker is an individual excursion that mirrors one's novel advantages, abilities, and vision for the computerized world.

Chapter 6

Redefining Celebrity and Fame

In the time of online entertainment and moment worldwide correspondence, the ideas of big name and distinction have gone through a significant change. The conventional way to fame, which once required long stretches of difficult work, devotion, and maybe a touch of karma, has been disturbed by the computerized age. This redefinition of big name and popularity has led to another type of forces to be reckoned with, web-based entertainment stars, and online sensations, testing how we might interpret being renowned.

Before, big names were commonly people who had accomplished an elevated degree of acknowledgment and reverence in their separate fields, like film, music, sports, or legislative issues. These famous people were frequently connected with a specific ability or expertise, and their distinction was worked over the long run through a blend of difficult work, ability, and the support of general society and media. They were the ones who graced magazine covers, strolled the red covers, and had their names in splendid lights.

However, in the 21st 100 years, the scene of big name has advanced. With the coming of web-based entertainment stages like Instagram,

YouTube, TikTok, and Twitter, anybody with a web association and a camera might possibly turn into a superstar short-term. This democratization of notoriety has obscured the lines between conventional superstars and regular people, prompting a redefinition of being renowned.

One of the principal traits of this new time of big name is the ascent of forces to be reckoned with. Powerhouses are people who have developed a significant following via virtual entertainment stages and influence their internet based presence to advance items, ways of life, or thoughts. They might not have the customary gifts or abilities that were once connected with VIP, yet they have the capacity to interface with their crowd on an individual level. Their acclaim is much of the time based on their appeal and legitimacy, making them more congenial and open than customary superstars.

Impact is currently a type of money in the computerized age, and powerhouses have become strong showcasing devices for brands and organizations. They can influence shopper conduct and effect mainstream society in manners that were recently held for Top notch VIPs. This change yet to be determined of force has led to another variety of VIPs who are renowned not really for their ability or accomplishments but rather for their capacity to impact and associate with their supporters.

Notwithstanding forces to be reckoned with, one more feature of the reclassified big name is the peculiarity of web-based entertainment stars. These are people who gain distinction basically through stages like TikTok, YouTube, or Instagram. They frequently make content that is diverting, engaging, or outwardly engaging, and their prosperity is estimated by the quantity of preferences, perspectives, and offers they get. Web-based entertainment stars have a worldwide reach, and their fan base can range across mainlands, making them in a split second unmistakable to a tremendous crowd.

The speed at which virtual entertainment stars can ascend to acclaim is surprising. A viral video or image can push a person from relative haziness to worldwide acknowledgment inside merely hours. This quick rising to popularity has prompted another degree of examination and strain on the people who end up at the center of attention. They should explore the difficulties of unexpected distinction, manage public analysis, and adjust to the requests of a computerized crowd that can whimsical and request.

The redefinition of VIP and popularity has additionally changed the conventional pathways to progress in fields like amusement and music. While ability and difficult work stay fundamental, they are presently not adequate all alone. Building an individual brand and developing areas of strength for a presence have become similarly significant. Artists, for instance, need to create excellent music as well as draw in with their crowd through virtual entertainment, live streaming, and online joint efforts. The capacity to interface with fans in a computerized space has turned into a significant part of current superstar.

One more part of this redefinition is the idea of "miniature famous people." These are people who might not have a huge number of supporters but rather have a devoted and drawn in specialty crowd. They are commended inside unambiguous networks or subcultures and can employ critical impact inside their picked space. While they may not be commonly recognized names, they are famous people by their own doing, with the ability to shape patterns and conclusions inside their specialty.

The coming of unscripted television shows has likewise assumed a critical part in reclassifying distinction. Unscripted television contenders, when conventional people, presently can possibly turn out to be mind-blowing phenomenons. The line between prearranged diversion and reality has obscured, and the show and validness of genuine circumstances have enamored crowds. This has made another variety of superstars who are renowned for acting naturally, no matter what.

As we ponder this redefinition of superstar and notoriety, taking into account both the positive and unfortunate results is fundamental. On the positive side, the democratization of acclaim has considered more assorted voices and stories to be heard. It has offered people from underestimated foundations the chance to share their encounters and points of view, testing the customary guards of media outlets. This inclusivity can possibly reshape cultural standards and separate generalizations.

Besides, web-based entertainment has empowered big names to connect straightforwardly with their fans, making a feeling of closeness and validness that was many times ailing before. VIPs can share their own lives, battles, and wins progressively, producing a more grounded association with their crowd. This straightforwardness can be enabling and encouraging to fans who consider their #1 superstars to be genuine individuals with interesting encounters.

On the negative side, the quest for distinction in the advanced age can adversely affect emotional well-being. The strain to keep an organized and cleaned web-based persona can prompt tension, wretchedness, and a consistent requirement for approval. Online badgering and analysis can negatively affect the psychological prosperity of those in the public eye, prompting a conundrum where the very stages that offer notoriety and fortune can likewise be wellsprings of individual trouble.

Besides, the journey for preferences, offers, and adherents can contort one's identity worth. It's not difficult to fall into the snare of estimating one's worth in view of online measurements, which can be transient and shallow. The quest for online distinction can likewise prompt a culture of correlation, where people continually measure their prosperity and prominence against others, frequently prompting insecurities.

The computerized age has additionally brought about the peculiarity of drop culture, where people who commit errors or offer disliked viewpoints are exposed to public judgment and segregation. While responsibility is fundamental, drop culture can be outrageous and unforgiving, frequently eclipsing the potential for development and reclamation.

Notwithstanding these difficulties, the redefinition of VIP has brought up issues about the worth of ability and mastery in a general public that frequently focuses on picture and persona. While powerhouses and online entertainment stars are without a doubt talented in the specialty of self-show, their notoriety can in some cases eclipse people who have committed their lives to dominating an art or expertise.

This change in center can have ramifications for the enthusiasm for genuine ability and aptitude.

Also, the adaptation of notoriety in the advanced age has prompted worries about validness and uprightness. Supported content and item supports are universal via web-based entertainment, and it tends to be trying to perceive when a singular's underwriting is authentic or driven by monetary motivating forces. This obscuring of lines among publicizing and individual suggestion can dissolve trust among famous people and their crowd.

The redefinition of superstar and distinction significantly affects the manner in which we consume media and diversion. Conventional news sources, like TV, magazines, and papers, have needed to adjust to the evolving scene. The ascent of virtual entertainment as an essential wellspring of information and diversion has upset the customary guardians of data. Today, anybody with a web association can communicate their perspectives, and this has prompted an expansion of elective voices and viewpoints.

The conventional limits among public and confidential life have likewise become progressively permeable in the computerized age. VIPs and individuals of note are presently expected to share a greater amount of their own lives, obscuring the lines between what is viewed as open and what is private. While this straightforwardness can cultivate a feeling of closeness, it can likewise prompt a deficiency of limits and a steady interruption into one's very own life.

The redefinition of superstar and popularity isn't restricted to the singular level yet additionally reaches out to the more extensive culture. The web and virtual entertainment have worked with the fast spread of patterns, thoughts, and developments, frequently determined by people who have acquired notoriety on the web. From viral provokes and hashtag developments to civil rights crusades and online activism, the force of computerized distinction can possibly drive huge social and social change.

In addition, the advanced age has led to the peculiarity of "web big names" who are popular principally for their internet based personas. These people might have various online entertainment accounts, each taking care of various parts of their personality. They frequently

curate an internet based picture that is painstakingly developed to speak to various interest groups. This compartmentalization of character can bring up issues about realness and the ease of personality in the advanced age.

The reclassified idea of VIP additionally meets with the issues of protection, reconnaissance, and information possession. As people share a greater amount of their lives on the web, they open themselves to expanded reconnaissance and information assortment by both privately owned businesses and legislatures. This trade of individual data for admittance to online stages raises worries about the disintegration of security and the potential for abuse of individual information.

Moreover, the commodification of notoriety in the advanced age has prompted worries about the typification of people, especially with regards to web-based entertainment and internet dating. The accentuation on picture and persona can decrease people to simple wares, made a decision about principally on their appearance and show. This commodification can damagingly affect confidence and self-perception, especially among youngsters who are experiencing childhood in the computerized age.

In the domain of governmental issues, the redefinition of superstar fundamentally affects how political missions are led. Legislators have become progressively mindful of the significance of developing areas of strength for a presence to interface with electors and shape general assessment. The utilization of online entertainment, live streaming, and computerized publicizing has become necessary to political informing, obscuring the lines among amusement and legislative issues.

Besides, political pioneers are not invulnerable to the traps of online acclaim. They also can become entangled in embarrassments, contention, and public examination, frequently enhanced by the persistent

24-hour consistent pattern of media reporting and web-based entertainment protected, closed off areas. The convergence of legislative issues and big name can prompt a sensationalization of political talk and an emphasis on character over strategy.

The re-imagined idea of big name likewise stretches out to the domain of charity and activism. VIPs and well known individuals are progressively utilizing their foundation to bring issues to light and assets for social and ecological causes. While this can have a positive effect, it likewise brings up issues about the job of VIP in friendly change. Is the emphasis on the big name's contribution eclipsing the significance of the main things? Is it true that we are depending too intensely because of people as opposed to resolving fundamental issues?

In the domain of craftsmanship and culture, the redefinition of superstar has tested customary thoughts of imaginative virtuoso. The capacity to make and share workmanship has never been more open, and specialists of all foundations and expertise levels can earn respect and a completely finishing online entertainment. This democratization of craftsmanship can possibly separate obstructions and advance assorted voices, yet it likewise brings up issues about the quality and credibility of imaginative articulation in the computerized age.

The redefinition of superstar and distinction significantly affects media outlets. Customary guardians, for example, record names, film studios, and distributing houses, are at this point not the sole referees of progress. Free craftsmen and makers can construct their professions and fan bases without the requirement for conventional delegates. This change in power has disturbed longstanding plans of action and tested how craftsmen are made up for their work.

Besides, the idea of distinction in the computerized age is profoundly entwined with the way of life of "virality." Content that becomes a web sensation, whether it's a video, an image, or a tweet, can move people to moment notoriety. The eccentricism of virality has made a culture of steady development and trial and error as people and brands look to cause the following viral situation. This fixation on virality can in some cases come to the detriment of profundity and substance in happy creation.

The reclassified idea of superstar has likewise led to the thought of "individual marking." People are progressively urged to organize and introduce a predictable picture and story of themselves on the web. This marking can be a two sided deal, taking into consideration self-articulation and realness, yet additionally bringing up issues about the strain to adjust to an attractive picture.

All in all, the redefinition of superstar and popularity in the computerized age is a mind boggling and diverse peculiarity. It has democratized popularity, permitting people from different foundations to earn respect and impact. It has likewise changed the manner in which we consume media, draw in with legislative issues, and associate with each other. Notwithstanding, this redefinition has carried with it a bunch of difficulties, remembering the effect for emotional well-being, the disintegration of protection, and the commodification of personality.

As we explore this advancing scene, it is urgent to analyze the ramifications of this reclassified idea of big name fundamentally. We should think about the consequences for society, culture, and the people who wind up at the center of attention. The computerized age has introduced another period of popularity, and it depends on us to shape it in a manner that mirrors our qualities and yearnings for what's in store.

6.1 The changing dynamics of fame in the digital era.

The computerized time has in a general sense changed the elements of distinction, reshaping how we see, accomplish, and communicate with it. The conventional pathways to acclaim, established in ability, accomplishment, and acknowledgment, have been upset and re-imagined by the unavoidable impact of the web, online entertainment, and computerized correspondence. This change has introduced another time of VIP and reconsidered being renowned.

The development of virtual entertainment stages, like Instagram, Twitter, Facebook, YouTube, and TikTok, plays had an essential impact in the changing elements of notoriety. These stages have democratized the method involved with earning respect and have obscured the lines between conventional superstars and ordinary people. Today, one's excursion to distinction can start with a straightforward post, tweet, or video that resounds with an expansive crowd. This newly discovered availability to popularity has prompted the ascent of powerhouses, virtual entertainment stars, and online sensations, rethinking the actual idea of VIP.

Forces to be reckoned with are people who have saddled the force of web-based entertainment to store up a critical following. Dissimilar to conventional superstars, forces to be reckoned with might not have a particular ability or expertise that recognizes them. All things being equal, their allure lies in their capacity to interface with their crowd on an individual level. They frequently share parts of their regular routines, offer way of life counsel, or advance items and brands, constructing a dedicated fan base all the while. Powerhouses use a novel type of computerized impact, molding customer conduct and patterns.

The ascent of forces to be reckoned with has tested the conventional idea of superstar, as it is not generally exclusively founded on perceived ability or accomplishment. In the computerized time, notoriety can be procured through credibility, appeal, and the capacity to resound with a specific interest group. The measurements of impact, like preferences, offers, and devotees, have turned into the money of acknowledgment, frequently eclipsing more traditional proportions of achievement.

Web-based entertainment stars, then again, gain notoriety essentially through unambiguous stages like TikTok, Instagram, or YouTube. They make content that is engaging, interesting, outwardly engaging, or provocative. A viral video or image can move a person from relative indefinite quality to worldwide acknowledgment inside merely hours. The speed at which online entertainment stars ascend to distinction is amazing and features the extraordinary force of computerized stages.

Right now worldwide reach has reclassified the idea of distinction. Web-based entertainment stars might have devotees from around the world, making them immediately conspicuous to a different and far reaching crowd. This interconnectedness has sped up the climb to popularity as well as set another degree of examination and strain on the people who wind up at the center of attention. They should explore the difficulties of unexpected distinction, adapt to public analysis, and adjust to the requests of a computerized crowd that can be both whimsical and requesting.

In the advanced period, progress in fields like amusement, music, and sports has additionally developed. While ability and difficult work stay fundamental, constructing an individual brand and developing areas of strength for a presence have become similarly significant. Artists, for example, need to create remarkable music as well as draw in with their crowd through web-based entertainment, live streaming, and online coordinated efforts. The capacity to interface with fans in a computerized space has turned into a pivotal part of current superstar.

Moreover, the idea of "miniature famous people" has arisen in the computerized time. These people might not have a huge number of supporters, but rather they have developed a committed and connected with specialty crowd. They are commended inside unambiguous networks or subcultures and can employ critical impact inside their picked space. While they may not be commonly recognized names, they are superstars by their own doing, molding patterns and feelings inside their specialty.

The redefinition of big name in the computerized time has both positive and adverse results. On the positive side, the democratization of distinction has took into consideration a more extensive portrayal of voices and stories. It has given people from assorted foundations and points of view the valuable chance to share their encounters, provoking customary guards and uncovering underestimated accounts. This inclusivity can possibly reshape cultural standards and separate generalizations.

Besides, web-based entertainment has empowered big names to connect straightforwardly with their fans, making a feeling of closeness and validness that was much of the time ailing before. Famous people can share their own lives, battles, and wins continuously, fashioning a more grounded association with their crowd. This straightforwardness can be engaging and consoling to fans who consider their #1 VIPs to be genuine individuals with appealing encounters.

Nonetheless, the quest for distinction in the computerized time isn't without its difficulties, especially in that frame of mind of psychological well-being. The strain to keep an organized and cleaned web-based persona can prompt uneasiness, misery, and a consistent requirement for approval. Online badgering and analysis can negatively affect the psychological prosperity of those in the public eye, prompting a mystery where the very stages that offer distinction and fortune can likewise be wellsprings of individual trouble.

Moreover, the mission for preferences, offers, and supporters can misshape one's healthy identity worth. It's not difficult to fall into the snare of estimating one's worth in view of online measurements, which can be brief and shallow. The quest for online notoriety can likewise prompt a culture of correlation, where people continually check their prosperity and fame against others, frequently prompting insecurities.

The computerized period has additionally brought about the peculiarity of "drop culture," where people who commit errors or offer disliked viewpoints are exposed to public judgment and exclusion. While responsibility is fundamental, drop culture can be outrageous and unforgiving, frequently eclipsing the potential for development and reclamation. The computerized age has made a culture where one's previous activities and proclamations can reemerge and torment them, possibly imperiling their profession and notoriety.

Notwithstanding these difficulties, the redefinition of VIP brings up issues about the worth of ability and mastery in a general public that frequently focuses on picture and persona. While forces to be reckoned with and web-based entertainment stars are without a doubt talented in the specialty of self-show, their notoriety can some of the time eclipse people who have devoted their lives to dominating an art or expertise.

This change in center can have ramifications for the enthusiasm for genuine ability and mastery.

Besides, the adaptation of acclaim in the advanced period has prompted worries about legitimacy and honesty. Supported content and item supports are omnipresent via virtual entertainment, and it very well may be trying to observe when a singular's underwriting is certified or driven by monetary motivators. This obscuring of lines among publicizing and individual suggestion can disintegrate trust among famous people and their crowd.

The redefinition of VIP in the computerized period has additionally changed the customary pathways to outcome in fields like diversion and music. The web has turned into a strong stage for arising craftsmen, permitting them to sidestep customary watchmen like record marks and contact their crowd straightforwardly. Free performers and content makers can fabricate a following and adapt their work without the requirement for delegates.

The computerized time has led to a culture of "DIY" notoriety, where people can make, advance, and disperse their work freely. This democratization of distinction has engaged specialists as well as extended the extent of innovativeness. Many voices and styles can thrive in the computerized scene, testing the predominance of traditional press and mainstream society.

Moreover, the idea of "web VIPs" has acquired noticeable quality in the computerized time. These people are renowned fundamentally for their web-based personas and may have numerous online entertainment accounts, each taking special care of various parts of their

personality. They frequently curate a web-based picture that is painstakingly developed to speak to various interest groups. This compartmentalization of personality can bring up issues about validness and the smoothness of character in the advanced age.

The redefinition of VIP in the advanced period crosses with the issues of security, observation, and information proprietorship. As people share a greater amount of their lives on the web, they open themselves to expanded observation and information assortment by both privately owned businesses and legislatures. This trade of individual data for admittance to online stages raises worries about the disintegration of security and the potential for abuse of individual information.

The commodification of acclaim in the advanced time likewise has sweeping impacts, stretching out past the domain of amusement. The fixation on picture and persona can penetrate different parts of life, especially with regards to web-based entertainment and internet dating. The accentuation on appearance and self-show can lessen people to simple wares, passed judgment on essentially on their visual allure and attractiveness. This commodification can damagingly affect confidence, self-perception, and the manner in which people see their value.

The computerized time has presented a huge change in political elements too. Political pioneers and up-and-comers have perceived the significance of developing areas of strength for a presence to interface with electors and shape popular assessment. The utilization of online entertainment, live streaming, and advanced promoting has become fundamental to political informing, obscuring the lines among amusement and governmental issues.

Moreover, the idea of "web VIPs" has acquired unmistakable quality in the computerized time. These people are well known principally for their web-based personas and may have various online entertainment accounts, each taking special care of various parts of their personality. They frequently curate an internet based picture that is painstakingly developed to engage different interest groups. This compartmentalization of personality can bring up issues about realness and the ease of character in the advanced age.

The redefinition of big name in the computerized period meets with the issues of protection, reconnaissance, and information proprietorship. As people share a greater amount of their lives on the web, they open themselves to expanded observation and information assortment by both privately owned businesses and states. This trade of individual data for admittance to online stages raises worries about the disintegration of security and the potential for abuse of individual information.

The commodification of distinction in the advanced period likewise has broad impacts, stretching out past the domain of amusement. The fixation on picture and persona can penetrate different parts of life, especially with regards to web-based entertainment and internet dating. The accentuation on appearance and self-show can lessen people to simple wares,

passed judgment on fundamentally on their visual allure and attractiveness. This commodification can damagingly affect confidence, self-perception, and the manner in which people see their value.

The computerized period has presented a huge change in political elements too. Political pioneers and competitors have perceived the significance of developing areas of strength for a presence to interface with electors and shape general assessment. The utilization of virtual entertainment, live streaming, and advanced publicizing has become basic to political informing, obscuring the lines among diversion and legislative issues.

As well as molding political talk, the advanced period has likewise led to political VIPs. These are people who gain distinction and impact principally through their association in political and social issues. The force of the web and virtual entertainment has permitted activists, analysts, and grassroots coordinators to fabricate enormous followings and influence general assessment. The crossing point of legislative issues and superstar can prompt a sensationalization of political talk and an emphasis on character over strategy.

The redefinition of superstar in the advanced time stretches out to altruism and activism too. Superstars and well known individuals are progressively utilizing their foundation to bring issues to light and assets for social and natural causes. While this can have a positive effect, it likewise brings up issues about the job of VIP in friendly change. Is the emphasis on the superstar's inclusion eclipsing the significance of the main things in need of attention? Is it true or not that we are depending too vigorously because of people as opposed to resolving fundamental issues?

In the domain of craftsmanship and culture, the computerized time has rethought the idea of creative virtuoso. The capacity to make and share craftsmanship has never been more open, and specialists of all foundations and expertise levels can earn respect and a finishing online entertainment. This democratization of craftsmanship can possibly separate obstructions and advance different voices, yet it likewise brings up issues about the quality and legitimacy of imaginative articulation in the computerized age.

The reclassified idea of VIP significantly affects media outlets. Customary guardians, for example, record names, film studios, and distributing houses, are presently not the sole authorities of accomplishment. Free craftsmen and makers can construct their vocations and fan bases without the requirement for customary mediators. This change in power has upset longstanding plans of action and tested how craftsmen are made up for their work.

The idea of virality is additionally intently attached to the changing elements of notoriety in the computerized time. Content that becomes famous online, whether it's a video, an image, or a tweet, can drive people to moment distinction. The capriciousness of virality has made a culture

of steady development and trial and error as people and brands try to cause the following viral situation. This fixation on virality can now and again come to the detriment of profundity and substance in happy creation.

6.2 The impact of viral content and online recognition.

The effect of viral substance and online acknowledgment in the computerized age is a complex peculiarity that has changed the manner in which we consume data, communicate our thoughts, and explore the steadily developing scene of the web. The capacity of content to turn into a web sensation, spreading quickly across online stages, has turned into a central quality of the computerized period. This peculiarity has reshaped the elements of notoriety as well as affected the manner in which we impart, collaborate, and even pursue choices in our regular routines.

Viral substance is described by its capacity to spread rapidly and broadly across the web. It can take many structures, from a hilarious video, a rousing statement, or a provocative article to an infectious image or a dazzling picture. Viral substance resounds with an expansive crowd, catching their consideration and inciting them to impart it to their own organizations. The course of content turning into a web sensation is in many cases unusual, driven by a blend of variables, including timing, significance, close to home effect, and shareability.

One of the main effects of viral substance is its capacity to shape public talk and impact mainstream society. A viral video, for instance, can present another dance frenzy, an expression, or a social test that catches the creative mind of millions. Images, specifically, have turned into an unavoidable type of viral substance, with pictures and subtitles that spread quickly and frequently take on a unique kind of energy. Images can be hilarious, ironical, or provocative, and they act as a common social cash in the computerized age.

Viral substance has likewise assumed a pivotal part in political and social developments. Hashtags, missions, and recordings have the ability to activate individuals, bring issues to light about significant issues, and drive certifiable change. Online entertainment stages have become landmarks for popular assessment and activism, with viral substance filling in as an incredible asset for those looking to rock the boat or promoter for a purpose. The #BlackLivesMatter development, for example, earned energy and far reaching respect through the viral spread of content that uncovered occurrences of police ruthlessness and foundational prejudice.

Notwithstanding its impact on mainstream society and social developments, viral substance has reshaped the media scene. Customary news sources are progressively dependent via virtual entertainment to source, report, and intensify viral stories. Reports, occasions, and patterns are in many cases driven by the virality of content, with columnists and news associations intently observing web-based entertainment to keep steady over arising stories. The capacity of people to become resident writers, catching and sharing news progressively, has upset the conventional gatekeeping job of the media.

In addition, the ascent of client created content, frequently as recordings and live streams, has obscured the lines between customary media and the substance delivered by people. Stages like YouTube, Jerk, and TikTok have made another age of content makers who can earn acclaim and respect through their interesting, credible, and frequently unfiltered content. The democratization of content creation has empowered people to construct crowds around their inclinations and interests, further growing the impact of viral substance.

The effect of viral substance stretches out to the domain of promoting and publicizing. Brands and organizations perceive the benefit of making content that can possibly become famous online. Viral advertising efforts expect to catch the consideration of people in general and influence the viral idea of content to increment brand perceivability and commitment. In any case, making viral substance is no simple accomplishment, as it requires a profound comprehension of the interest group, the capacity to take advantage of social patterns, and a portion of imagination. A fruitful viral mission can essentially help a memorability's and, at times, lead to expanded deals.

The predominance of viral substance significantly affects individual substance makers and powerhouses. Stages like YouTube and TikTok have permitted normal people to become computerized stars, bringing in cash through promotions, sponsorships, and product. For some, the fantasy about turning into an internet based content maker or powerhouse is driven by the charm of acknowledgment and the potential for monetary profit. While the existence of a powerhouse might seem marvelous, it accompanies its own arrangement of difficulties, including the strain to continually create connecting with content, deal with a web-based presence, and keep a dedicated following.

Besides, the journey for viral substance has made a culture of trial and error and inventiveness. Content makers, forces to be reckoned with, and advertisers constantly look for imaginative ways of catching the consideration of a computerized crowd. This drive for advancement has prompted the improvement of new happy organizations, narrating methods, and commitment methodologies. It has likewise changed the manner in which we see and consume diversion, with a developing accentuation on short-structure, outwardly captivating substance.

Nonetheless, the quest for viral substance can likewise have potentially negative results. The persevering spotlight on making content that becomes a web sensation can some of the time lead to a shallow and shallow way to deal with online correspondence. Content makers might focus on shock esteem, misleading content, and drama over profundity and realness with an end goal to catch the temporary consideration of online crowds. This race for viral acknowledgment has brought up issues about the effect of online notoriety on satisfied quality and cultural qualities.

The job of calculations and web-based entertainment stages in the spread of viral substance can't be undervalued. Calculations utilized by stages like Facebook, Instagram, and TikTok are intended to distinguish and advance substance that is probably going to connect with clients. These calculations consider client conduct, inclinations, and cooperations to arrange the substance that shows up on individual feeds. Basically, they assume a critical part in figuring out what becomes famous online and what gets covered in the computerized commotion.

The viral idea of content has likewise reclassified the idea of "fleeting encounter with notoriety," a term begat by craftsman Andy Warhol. In the computerized age, anybody might possibly accomplish a snapshot of popularity through a viral video or image. This short lived popularity can be both thrilling and testing. People who experience abrupt acknowledgment might have to explore the difficulties of public consideration, including on the web provocation, investigation, and the strain to keep up with importance.

The possibility of viral substance brings up issues about the worth of prevalence and acknowledgment in the advanced age. With a huge number of content pieces competing for focus, the measurements of preferences, offers, and perspectives can turn into the essential proportions of progress. The quest for online acknowledgment can possibly move the concentration from individual satisfaction and significant substance creation to a persistent race for numbers and virality.

Viral substance additionally affects our capacities to focus. The consistent stream of data and content in the computerized age has prompted abbreviated capacities to focus, with people rapidly looking at their feeds looking for the following drawing in piece of content. This peculiarity has suggestions for the manner in which we consume news, data, and even participate in longer-structure content like books and articles.

Besides, the viral spread of content can at times bring about deception and the fast dispersal of bogus or deceiving data. Falsehood can have serious outcomes, affecting popular assessment, molding political talk, and in any event, affecting general wellbeing. The viral idea of online substance enhances the difficulties of fighting deception, as bogus stories can spread more rapidly than reality actually looking at endeavors.

In the computerized age, the effect of viral substance is intently attached to the idea of "drop culture." Content that reemerges from a person's past or hostile assertions made online can prompt public judgment and social alienation. The capacity of viral substance to consider people responsible for their activities has brought up issues about the morals of online vigilantism and the potential for unnecessary discipline.

While the effect of viral substance and online acknowledgment is obvious, perceiving both the positive and unfortunate results of this phenomenon is fundamental. Viral substance can possibly engage, move, illuminate, and activate. It can reveal insight into significant social and policy driven issues, present new voices and viewpoints, and challenge customary watchmen of data and culture. Viral substance has the ability to join individuals around a typical reason and drive social change.

Be that as it may, the quest for virality can likewise unfavorably affect content quality, individual qualities, and mental prosperity. The way of life of "becoming famous online" can possibly focus on triviality, melodrama, and shock esteem over profundity and realness. It can prompt an obsession with numbers and measurements, cultivating a culture of examination and contest. Viral substance can now and again sustain negative generalizations, propagate deception, and fuel online provocation and drop culture.

As we explore the computerized scene, it is urgent to survey the effect of viral substance and online acknowledgment fundamentally. We should think about the job of calculations, stages, and content makers in forming the viral biological system. We should likewise consider the worth we put on acknowledgment and notoriety in the computerized age and what it means for our ways of behaving and perspectives. Viral substance is a situation with two sides, and its effect on our general public and culture will keep on developing as the computerized period unfurls. It depends on us to shape where it takes and to bridle its true capacity for positive change.

7

Chapter 7

Balancing Act: Screen Time and Well-being

Adjusting screen time and prosperity has turned into an undeniably mind boggling and imperative issue in the computerized age. As innovation keeps on propelling, our lives have become more interlaced with screens, from cell phones and tablets to PCs and TVs. While screens have brought colossal advantages, empowering correspondence, admittance to data, and diversion, they have likewise raised worries about the possible effect on our psychological and actual wellbeing. Accomplishing a harmony between our screen time and generally prosperity is a test that requires a more profound comprehension of the main things and an insightful way to deal with dealing with our computerized lives.

The expansion of screens in our day to day routines is unquestionable. The appearance of cell phones has made admittance to the advanced world ever-present, permitting us to remain associated with loved ones, access work messages, and take part in virtual entertainment anyplace and whenever. PCs and PCs have become fundamental devices for work, training, and relaxation. TV screens keep on being an essential wellspring of diversion, offering a huge swath of shows, films, and content. The rise of new innovations, like computer generated simulation and increased the truth, is further obscuring the limits between the physical and advanced universes.

The unavoidable idea of screens has prompted an expansion in screen time for individuals, everything being equal. Kids and youths, specifically, are experiencing childhood in a computerized scene, where screens are important for their ordinary schedules. The ramifications of this consistent openness to screens possibly affect actual wellbeing, emotional wellness, and generally prosperity.

Actual wellbeing concerns related with unreasonable screen time incorporate the gamble of stationary way of behaving and its related medical conditions. Drawn out screen time frequently prompts a more stationary way of life, with people burning through broadened periods sitting or resting. This absence of active work can add to medical problems like stoutness, cardiovascular sickness, and outer muscle issues. Besides, unreasonable screen time, particularly when it impedes rest designs, can prompt disturbances in circadian rhythms, which thusly influence generally wellbeing.

The connection between screen time and emotional well-being is one more area of concern. A few investigations have proposed an association between inordinate screen time, especially via virtual entertainment stages, and expanded sensations of uneasiness, misery, and depression. The consistent openness to arranged, glorified portrayals of others' lives via virtual entertainment can cultivate social examination and adversely influence confidence. Furthermore, the moment satisfaction and dopamine-driven criticism circles found in numerous advanced applications and games can add to habit-forming ways of behaving and elevated feelings of anxiety.

One of the striking worries with respect to screen time is its effect on kids and youths. Unreasonable screen time in these age gatherings can prompt formative issues. It might slow down the advancement of social and close to home abilities, as computerized collaborations may not give similar profundity of understanding and sympathy as eye to eye connections. It can likewise influence the advancement of consideration and leader working, as steady openness to screens and performing multiple tasks might prevent mental turn of events.

Also, youngsters and teenagers are more defenseless against the substance they experience on the web. Openness to savage, sexual, or improper material can lastingly affect their mental prosperity. The potential for cyberbullying and online provocation represents extra dangers to their emotional wellness and can prompt sensations of detachment and misery.

The screen time and prosperity banter isn't restricted to the more youthful age; grown-ups are likewise wrestling with these difficulties. The requests of work in the computerized age frequently require delayed screen time, which can prompt burnout, stress, and an obscured limit among work and individual life. The steady availability empowered by cell phones implies that individuals are every now and again browsing messages and messages beyond working hours, making it trying to completely separate and unwind.

Besides, the computerized age has achieved a culture of data overburden. The consistent progression of information, updates, and content can add to sensations of overpower and uneasiness. The every minute of every day consistent pattern of media reporting and the strain to remain informed can negatively affect psychological wellness, as people might encounter an increased feeling of dread, vulnerability, and data weariness.

Adjusting screen time and prosperity is a mind boggling try, however it isn't impossible. The critical lies in embracing a careful and deliberate way to deal with our computerized utilization. This approach includes mindfulness, informed decisions, and the execution of methodologies to enhance our screen time for positive results.

One of the central parts of accomplishing a good overall arrangement between screen time and prosperity is mindfulness. Understanding the effect of screens on our physical and psychological wellness is a significant initial step. Self-evaluation can assist people with perceiving examples of screen use, distinguish expected wellsprings of pain, and settle on informed conclusions about their computerized propensities. It is critical to occasionally assess what screen time means for rest, feelings of anxiety, mind-set, and by and large prosperity.

When mindfulness is laid out, people can settle on informed decisions about their screen time. This might include defining clear limits and objectives for advanced utilization. For instance, people can assign explicit times for browsing and answering messages, apportion time for sporting screen use, and lay out "no-screen" zones in the home, like the room or eating region. The utilization of computerized apparatuses, for example, screen time following applications and implicit gadget highlights, can likewise help people screen and deal with their screen time.

With regards to kids and young people, guardians and parental figures assume a basic part in defining limits and teaching them about capable screen use. It is fundamental to lay out age-fitting rules and screen the substance kids are presented to. Empowering disconnected exercises, like actual activity, perusing, and eye to eye social collaborations, can assist with advancing a decent and sound way of life.

A significant part of overseeing screen time is the nature of content consumed. Not everything screen time is made equivalent. Instructive substance, imaginative pursuits, and content that encourages significant associations with others can decidedly affect prosperity. Then again, thoughtless looking over and unreasonable openness to sensationalized news and web-based entertainment can add to pressure and tension. Consequently, people ought to endeavor to organize their advanced surroundings by choosing excellent substance that lines up with their inclinations and values.

To figure out some kind of harmony between screen time and prosperity, people ought to focus on advanced detoxes and snapshots of computerized disengagement. These times of turning off from screens can assist people with re-energizing, pull together, and reconnect with the actual world. Straightforward practices, like enjoying reprieves to stretch, walk, or practice care, can give genuinely necessary help from steady advanced openness. Also, consolidating outside exercises and leisure activities that don't include screens can upgrade in general prosperity and psychological wellness.

The administration of screen time ought to likewise incorporate methodologies for improving the nature of rest. Blue light produced by screens can upset rest designs, so laying out a computerized time limitation basically an hour prior to bedtime is prudent. This permits the body to slow down and plan for tranquil rest. Besides, establishing a rest helpful climate by limiting screen use in the room, keeping a reliable rest plan, and rehearsing unwinding methods can further develop rest quality.

With regards to the working environment, managers can assume a critical part in advancing a good overall arrangement between screen time and prosperity. Empowering clear limits among work and individual time, as well as giving chances to breaks and active work, can diminish burnout and further develop representative prosperity. Organizations can likewise offer preparation and assets to assist representatives with overseeing computerized pressure and keep a sound balance between fun and serious activities.

The effect of screen time on kids and youths is a point that requires exceptional consideration. Guardians and teachers ought to plan to find some kind of harmony between screen-based learning and proactive tasks that help advancement. Empowering decisive reasoning and media proficiency can assist youthful people with exploring the computerized scene and recognize dependable data from deception. Parental direction and open correspondence with youngsters about dependable screen use are fundamental parts of guaranteeing their prosperity.

7.1 Concerns and challenges related to excessive screen time.

Over the top screen time, driven by the multiplication of computerized gadgets and the digitalization of different parts of our lives, has raised a large group of worries and difficulties that influence our physical, mental, and social prosperity. While screens have reformed correspondence, diversion, and work, the abuse of computerized gadgets has prompted a scope of issues, from medical conditions to changes in our social texture. In this conversation, we will investigate the various worries and difficulties related with unnecessary screen time and the ramifications for people and society in general.

1. **Actual Wellbeing Concerns:**
1. **Inactive Way of life:** Unnecessary screen time frequently prompts a stationary way of life. Hours spent sitting before screens, whether for work, amusement, or associating, can add to different medical conditions, including heftiness, cardiovascular issues, and outer muscle inconvenience. Absence of active work, related to delayed screen time, is a critical worry, as it lessens energy use and effects in general wellness.

2. **Advanced Eye Strain:** Delayed screen use can bring about computerized eye strain or PC vision condition. This condition includes side effects, for example, dry eyes, eye weariness, cerebral pains, and obscured vision. The drawn out timeframes spent gazing at screens, frequently at close distances, can prompt eye uneasiness and visual issues.

3. **Unfortunate Rest Examples:** Screens, especially those of cell phones and tablets, produce blue light, which can disrupt rest designs. Openness to blue light, particularly at night, upsets the body's development of melatonin, a chemical that directs rest. Unfortunate rest can bring about weariness, decreased focus, and expanded powerlessness to different medical conditions.

4. **Radiation Concerns:** Albeit the proof is uncertain, a few people stress over the potential wellbeing impacts of electromagnetic radiation discharged by screens. This worry is especially significant for drawn out and short proximity openness, as on account of cell phones and workstations.

2. **Emotional well-being Difficulties:**

1. **Tension and Stress:** The steady network managed by screens, including admittance to messages, online entertainment, and news refreshes, can possibly create uneasiness and stress. The strain to be consistently accessible, answer speedily, or remain informed can prompt increased degrees of tension and a feeling of being overpowered.

2. **Gloom and Dejection:** Exploration has proposed that unnecessary screen time, especially via virtual entertainment, might be connected to higher paces of sadness and depression. Exorbitant utilization of virtual entertainment stages can cultivate social examination and lead to insecurities and depression.

3. **Dependence and Habitual Ways of behaving:** Screen time, especially when related with computer games, virtual entertainment, or web based betting, can prompt habit-forming and urgent ways of behaving. The moment satisfaction and dopamine-driven rewards found in these computerized encounters can be propensity framing and lead to a decreased personal satisfaction.

4. **Disabled Mental Turn of events:** In kids and young people, exorbitant screen time can adversely affect mental turn of events. The consistent commitment with screens, performing multiple tasks, and the predominance of moment satisfaction can prevent the improvement of consideration and leader capabilities.

3. Social and Relationship Difficulties:

1. **Decreased Up close and personal Connection:** The utilization of screens for correspondence, for example, messaging and video calls, has prompted a decrease in eye to eye communications. In-person friendly cooperations are fundamental for building and keeping up with significant connections, and a decrease here of commitment can make negative social impacts.

2. **Family and Relationship Strain:** Unnecessary screen time inside families can prompt relationship strain. At the point when

relatives spend a significant part of their time drew in with screens, it can diminish the nature of family collaborations and obstruct the improvement of solid family bonds.

3. **Social Disengagement:** While screens offer the deception of social association, unreasonable screen time can add to social segregation. Investing more energy drawing in with screens and less time in actual organization can prompt sensations of forlornness and separation from certifiable interpersonal organizations.

4. Protection and Security Concerns:

1. **Protection Attack:** With the rising utilization of advanced gadgets and the web, worries about security intrusion have developed. Information breaks, unapproved access, and individual data spillage are issues that people should fight with. The additional time spent on the web, the more noteworthy the openness to potential protection chances.

2. **Online protection Dangers:** Over the top screen time, especially in the event that it includes perusing the web and drawing in with different computerized stages, builds the gamble of experiencing network safety dangers. These dangers can go from malware and phishing tricks to data fraud and monetary misrepresentation.

5. Diminished Efficiency:

1. **Work and Scholastic Execution:** Unnecessary screen time, especially when utilized for non-useful exercises like web-based entertainment or gaming, can adversely influence work and scholarly execution. Tarrying and interruptions originating from extreme screen use can upset efficiency and accomplishment.

6. Online Badgering and Tormenting:

1. **Cyberbullying:** The internet based world can be a favorable place for cyberbullying, provocation, and dangers. Exorbitant screen time might uncover people, particularly youngsters and teenagers, to the gamble of online maltreatment, which can make significant mental impacts.

7. Influence on Capacity to focus:

1. **Diminished Capacity to focus:** Extreme screen time, portrayed by speedy and regular movements of consideration, may add to an abbreviated capacity to focus. This is especially unsettling for youngsters and youths, as it can influence their scholastic exhibition and capacity to center.

8. Data Over-burden:

1. **Overpower:** The consistent progression of data, news updates, and content on screens can bring about data over-burden. This persistent stream of information might prompt sensations of overpower and tension, as people battle to stay aware of the volume of data.

9. Changes in Accepted practices:

1. **Social Behavior:** Unreasonable screen time has tested conventional accepted practices and manners. The utilization of cell phones during supper, during gatherings, or in parties has become progressively normal, affecting the nature of in-person cooperations and possibly prompting an absence of graciousness.

10. The "Apprehension about Passing up a major opportunity" (FOMO):

1. **Nervousness About Prohibition:** The pervasiveness of screens, online entertainment, and constant updates has led to a peculiarity known as the "anxiety toward passing up a great opportunity" (FOMO). People might encounter uneasiness about being barred from get-togethers or discussions on the off chance that they are not continually associated.

The worries and difficulties related with extreme screen time are complicated and complex, influencing people of any age and cultural designs. Resolving these issues requires an extensive methodology that includes mindfulness, self-guideline, and the foundation of clear limits for computerized utilization. The effect of screen time on physical and emotional well-being, social communications, and by and large prosperity highlights the significance of tending to these difficulties proactively and in a decent way.

Moreover, there is a developing requirement for computerized proficiency and schooling to help people, particularly youngsters, explore the computerized scene capably. Empowering computerized detoxes, active work, and up close and personal social collaborations can add to a better and more offset relationship with screens. Eventually, it is urgent for people to assume responsibility for their screen time and pursue informed choices that focus on their prosperity and the prosperity of everyone around them. Adjusting the advantages of screen innovation with the difficulties it presents is a basic part of carrying on with a satisfying and sound life in the computerized age.

7.2 Strategies for maintaining a healthy balance.

Procedures for keeping a good arrangement in the computerized age are fundamental for address the worries and difficulties related with over the top screen time. While screens have turned into a fundamental piece of our lives, significant to embrace practices and methods advance prosperity and guarantee that our computerized utilization serves our physical, mental, and social requirements. In this conversation, we will investigate a scope of techniques that people and society can utilize to keep a good overall arrangement in their screen time.

1. **Lay out Clear Computerized Limits:**
   One of the essential methodologies for accomplishing a good overall arrangement is to lay out clear computerized limits. This includes drawing explicit lines on when, where, and how screens are utilized. For instance:

   No-Screen Zones: Assign specific region of the home, like the room or lounge area, as "no-screen zones." These regions ought to be saved for exercises that don't include screens, like perusing, dinners, or discussions.

   Without screen Times: Assign explicit times during the day when screens are not permitted. For example, laying out a "without screen hour" before sleep time can assist with further developing rest quality by diminishing openness to blue light.

   Screen-Time Cutoff points: Carry out everyday or week after week screen-time limits for various exercises. For instance, put forth a greatest line for sporting screen use or video gaming. A few gadgets and applications offer implicit elements to assist screen and control with screening time.

2. **Focus on Actual work:**
   To battle the inactive way of life related with inordinate screen time, focusing on actual work is fundamental. Standard activity advances actual wellbeing as well as supports mental prosperity. Systems include:

   Booked Actual work: Put away opportunity every day for actual activity, whether it's strolling, running, cycling, or taking part in sports. Laying out a standard guarantees reliable actual work.

   Dynamic Breaks: Consolidate short, dynamic breaks into your screen time. Stand up, stretch, and move around each hour, especially during work or study meetings. These breaks can assist with diminishing the adverse consequence of delayed sitting.

Open air Exercises: Take part in outside exercises that include nature and outside air. Exercises like climbing, planting, or playing sports in the recreation area give a break from screens and an association with the actual world.

3. **Curate Your Computerized Climate:**

The nature of content consumed on screens fundamentally influences prosperity. Arranging your computerized climate includes choosing excellent substance that lines up with your inclinations and values while limiting openness to negative or time-squandering content:

Unfollow and Withdraw: Routinely survey your virtual entertainment and online memberships. Unfollow or withdraw from records or channels that don't enhance your life or add to pessimistic feelings.

Specific News Utilization: Pick dependable hotspots for news utilization and breaking point how much time spent on news refreshes. Stay away from the consistent invigorating of news sources, which can prompt data over-burden and tension.

Instructive Substance: Decide on instructive and educational substance that lines up with your inclinations and objectives. Stages like YouTube offer an abundance of instructive channels that give learning open doors.

4. **Execute Computerized Detoxes:**

Occasional computerized detoxes are fundamental for keeping a good arrangement. These detoxes include enjoying some time off from screens to re-energize, center around proactive tasks, and reconnect with the actual world:

Booked Detoxes: Plan standard computerized detoxes, like ends of the week or explicit days of the week, where you shun involving evaluates for superfluous exercises.

Gadget Free Excursions: While taking get-aways, think about abandoning computerized gadgets or utilizing them sparingly. Center around submerging yourself in the encounters and environmental factors.

Detox from Explicit Stages: In the event that you track down that a specific stage or application is consuming a lot of your time and adversely influencing your prosperity, consider a detox from that stage explicitly.

5. **Careful Screen Use:**

Care is a significant methodology for overseeing screen time. Careful screen use includes being completely present and aware of your advanced cooperations, as opposed to participating in thoughtless or urgent ways of behaving:

Computerized Goal Setting: Prior to drawing in with screens, set a reasonable expectation for what you need to accomplish. Whether it's browsing messages, making up for lost time with news, or interfacing with companions, having a reason forestalls random looking over.

Careful Utilization: Focus on the substance you consume and your profound responses. Assuming you find that specific substance inspires pessimistic feelings or consumes inordinate time, reconsider your utilization designs.

Planned Screen Time: Distribute explicit times for screen use, especially for exercises like browsing messages or online entertainment. Adhere to the timetable, and when your assigned time is finished, withdraw from screens.

6. **Upgrade Rest Cleanliness:**

To counter the effect of screens on rest designs, it's essential to lay out great rest cleanliness rehearses. These practices add to all the more likely rest quality and generally speaking prosperity:

Screen Check in time: Execute a screen time limit, normally an hour prior to sleep time. During this time, keep away from screens to decrease openness to blue light that can disturb rest.

Room Rejection: Keep screens out of the room to establish a climate helpful for rest. The room ought to be saved for rest and unwinding.

Unwinding Procedures: Practice unwinding methods, like contemplation or profound breathing activities, before sleep time to advance a feeling of quiet and further develop rest quality.

7. **Urge Up close and personal Cooperations:**
Adjusting screen time includes encouraging significant eye to eye collaborations and connections. These collaborations are fundamental for social prosperity:

Quality Time: Put away quality time for eye to eye connections with companions, family, and friends and family. Participate in exercises that advance genuine associations.

Sans tech Get-togethers: While meeting companions or going to parties, urge without tech zones to guarantee that everybody is completely present and participated in the occasion.

8. **Computerized Proficiency and Training:**
Computerized proficiency and training are essential for people of any age, especially youngsters and youths. They ought to be outfitted with the abilities and information to mindfully explore the advanced scene:

Media Proficiency: Instruct people, particularly youngsters, about media education. Train them to fundamentally assess online substance, observe valid data, and perceive the effect of media on their discernments and convictions.

Online Security: Bring issues to light about web-based wellbeing and the expected dangers of over the top screen time. Stress the significance of security settings, solid passwords, and detailing systems for online badgering or cyberbullying.

9. **Support Disconnected Exercises:**
Advancing disconnected exercises is fundamental for keeping a good arrangement. These exercises connect with people in true encounters and give a break from screens:

Perusing: Energize perusing actual books or magazines. Perusing gives significant information as well as cultivates innovativeness and creative mind.

Leisure activities: Seek after leisure activities and interests that don't include screens. Whether it's painting, playing an instrument, or participating in sports, side interests give a feeling of satisfaction and pleasure.

Open air Investigation: Invest energy in nature, whether it's climbing, planting, or basically partaking in a stroll in the park. Outside exercises offer a reprieve from screens and an association with the actual world.

10. **Open Correspondence:**

Successful correspondence, especially inside families, is critical for overseeing screen time. Transparent discussions about advanced propensities and their effect on prosperity can prompt more mindful and adjusted screen use:

Family Conversations: Start conversations inside the family about screen time rules and assumptions. Include relatives in setting and keeping up with these standards.

Normal Registrations: Occasionally check in with relatives about their screen time propensities. Talk about any worries or difficulties that might have emerged.

11. **Enable Bosses:**

Managers can assume a part in elevating a reasonable way to deal with screen time. By empowering strategies and practices that help representative prosperity, organizations can add to a better balance between serious and fun activities:

Adaptable Work Courses of action: Consider offering adaptable work game plans that permit representatives to all the more likely deal with their computerized balance between serious and fun activities. This might incorporate choices for remote work, adaptable hours, or assigned "disconnected" hours.

Work-Life Limits: Energize clear limits among work and individual time. Encourage representatives to separate from business related screens beyond working hours to forestall burnout.

12. **Advocate for Computerized Prosperity:**
    People and associations can advocate for computerized prosperity and bring issues to light of the significance of keeping a good arrangement:
    Local area Drives: Backing and take part in local area drives or missions that advance capable screen use, particularly for youngsters and youths.
    Instructive Projects: Support the turn of events and execution of instructive projects on computerized prosperity in schools and local area associations.
13. **Look for Proficient Assistance When Required:**

For people battling with unreasonable screen time and its related difficulties, looking for proficient assistance might be important. Psychological wellness experts, advisors, and instructors can give direction and backing to address habit-forming ways of behaving, nervousness, discouragement, or other emotional well-being issues connected with screen time.

Chapter 8

The Ongoing Technological Evolution

The continuous mechanical development is a persistent power that has formed human culture in significant and complex ways. Starting from the commencement of the primary stone devices and fire-production, our species has been on a continuous mission to outfit and control the climate to address our issues and wants. This mission has brought forth a nonstop pattern of development, wherein every disclosure and progression prompts additional opportunities and difficulties. Throughout the long term, we have seen the ascent and fall of incalculable advancements, from the print machine to the web, each transforming mankind's set of experiences.

In the cutting edge time, the speed of mechanical development has advanced quickly to a remarkable degree. It's anything but a misrepresentation to say that we are living in a period of fast and extraordinary change. In this exposition, we will investigate the critical drivers and results of this continuous mechanical development, addressing its effect on different parts of human existence, from the manner in which we work and convey to how we comprehend and control the actual world.

One of the focal drivers of the innovative development is the persistent quest for effectiveness. From the Modern Upset to the computerized age, the mission to accomplish more with less has been a characterizing element of mechanical advancement. This drive for effectiveness has brought about incalculable developments, from mechanical production systems and computerization to calculations and man-made reasoning. These developments have reshaped ventures and economies as well as reclassified the idea of work itself.

Mechanization and man-made consciousness, specifically, are upsetting the labor force. Assignments that were once performed by people are currently being executed by machines and calculations, prompting worries about work dislodging and the fate of work. While some contend that these advances will set out new open doors and occupations, the change isn't generally smooth, and differences in schooling and admittance to preparing can compound disparity. Also, as simulated intelligence keeps on propelling, the subject of the moral utilization of these innovations turns out to be progressively significant. Issues like predisposition in calculations and the potential for independent weapons raise basic moral quandaries.

The effect of innovative development isn't restricted to the work environment; it reaches out to each feature of day to day existence. The manner in which we convey and associate with each other has been decisively changed by the coming of the web and portable innovation. Virtual entertainment, specifically, has turned into a pervasive piece of current presence, changing the manner in which we structure connections, share data, and draw in with the world. It has made additional opportunities for worldwide correspondence and activism, while likewise raising worries about protection, falsehood, and the disintegration of common talk.

The field of medical care is another space where innovative development is having a significant effect. Progresses in clinical innovation, like genomics, telemedicine, and automated a medical procedure, are working on persistent consideration and expanding futures. These advancements likewise present moral problems connected with hereditary security, the expense of medical services, and the potential for dehumanization in medication. Also, the crossing point of innovation and medical services has led to the field of biohacking, where people look to improve their own bodies and brains using inserts, nootropics, and other arising advancements.

The continuous innovative advancement is likewise reshaping our relationship with the climate. While innovation has generally been a driver of ecological debasement, it is presently being bridled to address the earnest difficulties of environmental change and maintainability. Environmentally friendly power sources, as sunlight based and wind power, are turning out to be progressively practical and inescapable, offering a way toward decreasing our dependence on petroleum derivatives. Furthermore, headways in energy capacity, transportation, and farming are adding to a more reasonable future.

The combination of innovation and manageability is additionally apparent in the ascent of the round economy, which looks to limit squander and advance the proficient utilization of assets. 3D printing, for instance, can possibly change fabricating by permitting items to be made on request, diminishing the requirement for large scale manufacturing and significant distance transportation. Additionally, the Web of Things (IoT) is empowering savvy frameworks that can streamline asset use, from energy-productive structures to accuracy horticulture.

The domain of amusement and culture has not been resistant to the effect of mechanical development. The digitization of media, from music and films to books and computer games, has changed how we consume and make content. Streaming stages have upset customary circulation models, furnishing purchasers with additional decisions and accommodation. Be that as it may, the ascent of computerized media has likewise brought up issues about licensed innovation, the job of craftsmen, and the potential for protected, closed off areas and deception in the advanced scene.

Virtual and increased reality advances are pushing the limits of vivid amusement encounters. These advances have applications past diversion, remembering for instruction, preparing, and treatment. In any case, they likewise suggest conversation starters about protection, habit, and the obscuring of the line between the virtual and actual universes.

In the field of schooling, the continuous mechanical advancement is reshaping the manner in which we learn and educate. Internet learning stages, virtual study halls, and instructive applications are growing admittance to schooling and taking into consideration customized opportunities for growth. Nonetheless, the computerized partition stays a huge test, with numerous understudies lacking admittance to the important innovation and web network. The fate of schooling should resolve issues of openness, quality, and the job of educators in an innovation driven learning climate.

Logical examination and revelation have likewise been significantly affected by the continuous innovative development. Elite execution figuring and enormous information examination are empowering forward leaps in fields as different as astronomy, genomics, and environment science. The capacity to process and dissect tremendous measures of information has opened new outskirts of information, however it has likewise raised worries about information security, protection, and the potential for algorithmic inclination.

The field of room investigation is encountering a renaissance, driven by headways in mechanical technology, impetus, and materials science. Privately owned businesses are assuming an undeniably critical part in space investigation, possibly prompting another time of business space travel and asset extraction. These advancements bring up issues about the administration of room, ecological effect, and the potential for struggle over extraterrestrial assets.

The continuous mechanical development is in a general sense changing our relationship with data and information. The web has democratized admittance to data, empowering people to become content makers and disseminators. This has the ability to challenge conventional orders of information and authority, yet it likewise raises worries about the spread of deception and the disintegration of decisive reasoning.

The coming of blockchain innovation can possibly upset the manner in which we store and trade esteem. Digital currencies like Bitcoin have disturbed conventional monetary frameworks, offering additional opportunities for monetary consideration and protection. In any case, they additionally bring up issues about guideline, security, and the potential for crimes in the advanced domain.

The improvement of quantum registering is not too far off, with the possibility to reform fields as different as cryptography, materials science, and medication revelation. Quantum registering's appearance may likewise challenge the security of current encryption techniques and lead to international changes in innovation and data fighting.

The continuous innovative development isn't exclusively a human undertaking. It is progressively obscuring the line among people and machines. The field of transhumanism investigates the combination of innovation with the human body, promising improvements in regions like life span, cognizance, and tactile discernment. In any case, this union brings up significant moral issues about the idea of human personality, independence, and the potential for social separation.

As innovation keeps on propelling, the limits between the virtual and actual universes are turning out to be progressively permeable. Increased reality, for instance, overlays computerized data onto the actual climate, offering additional opportunities for route, gaming, and instruction. The improvement of the metaverse, an aggregate virtual shared space, can possibly change how we mingle, work, and lead business. This obscuring of limits can possibly alter how we communicate with the world, yet it additionally brings up issues about security, personality, and the potential for habit.

The continuous innovative advancement is likewise affecting the domain of administration and international relations. The ascent of digital fighting and the weaponization of data have made new outskirts of contention and reconnaissance. Countries are wrestling with the need to foster procedures for safeguarding basic foundation and getting their advanced lines. The appearance of independent weapons and the potential for algorithmic dynamic in military activities bring up significant moral and legitimate issues about the eventual fate of fighting.

The transaction of innovation and governmental issues is clear in the ascent of observation states and worries about security and common freedoms. The multiplication of facial acknowledgment innovation and the assortment of tremendous measures of information on people bring up issues about the harmony among security and individual flexibility. Also, the job of web-based entertainment in molding general assessment and political talk has raised worries about the impact of innovation on majority rules government and the potential for data control.

The continuous mechanical advancement is likewise changing the scene of development itself. Open-source programming, cooperative stages, and worldwide organizations of specialists are democratizing the course of development. Publicly supporting and crowdfunding are empowering people and little gatherings to finance and foster inventive activities. This change can possibly speed up the speed of revelation and expand admittance to development, yet it likewise brings up issues about licensed innovation, guideline, and the job of conventional foundations in the advancement environment.

The improvement of independent vehicles is ready to upset transportation, promising more secure and more productive versatility. Notwithstanding, it likewise brings up issues about the effect on positions in the transportation area, the morals of machine direction, and the rethinking of metropolitan spaces.

The continuous mechanical development is interlaced with the difficulties of online protection. As our dependence on innovation extends, so does the potential for cyberattacks and information breaks. The requirement for vigorous network safety measures and the advancement of secure innovations are of vital significance to safeguard people, associations, and legislatures from pernicious entertainers.

The continuous innovative development isn't without its quandaries and compromises. While it offers the potential for remarkable advancement and human improvement, it likewise presents difficulties and dangers that require smart and moral thought. The double use nature of numerous advances implies that they can be utilized for both gainful and unsafe purposes. The mindful turn of events and utilization of innovation are basic in tending to these moral quandaries.

One of the overall inquiries in the continuous mechanical development is the job of morals and values in directing its direction. As we stand at the limit of a future where innovation can reshape the human involvement with ways beforehand incomprehensible, taking into account the moral ramifications of our actions is fundamental. This incorporates inquiries concerning the fair appropriation of the advantages of innovation, the assurance of individual privileges and protection, the evasion of damage to society and the climate, and the safeguarding of human respect despite fast change.

The continuous innovative development likewise brings up issues about the connection among people and machines. As computerized reasoning and mechanization keep on propelling, we should wrestle with the likely dislodging of occupations and the redefinition of the human job in the labor force. This shift might expect us to reevaluate the idea of work, schooling, and the social wellbeing net to guarantee that people can flourish in a world progressively formed by machines.

The fate of innovation additionally holds the potential for extraordinary forward leaps in fields like biotechnology, nanotechnology, and materials science. These advancements can possibly expand human capacities, fix sicknesses, and address squeezing worldwide difficulties. In any case, they additionally present moral and security worries that require cautious oversight and guideline.

The subject of how to oversee and manage innovation is a squeezing one. In a globalized reality where innovation knows no lines, accomplishing agreement on moral principles and administrative structures can challenge. Global collaboration is vital for address issues like information security, network safety, and the mindful utilization of arising innovations. The pressure among development and guideline is a sensitive equilibrium that social orders should strike.

The continuous innovative development additionally brings up issues about the job of training and advanced proficiency. As innovation keeps on shaping our lives, people should foster the abilities and information to actually explore the computerized scene. This incorporates decisive reasoning, media proficiency, and a comprehension of the moral ramifications of innovation. The eventual fate of schooling should focus on these abilities to plan people for the difficulties and chances of an innovation driven world.

All in all, the continuous mechanical development is a dynamic and extraordinary power that is reshaping each part of human life. It is driven by the persistent quest for productivity, the combination of people and machines, and the obscuring of limits between the virtual and actual universes. The effect of innovation stretches out from the manner in which we work and impart to how we comprehend and control the actual world.

While the continuous mechanical advancement offers phenomenal opportunities for progress and human improvement, it additionally presents significant moral and cultural difficulties. The capable turn of events and utilization of innovation, the fair circulation of its advantages, and the security of individual freedoms and protection are among the squeezing moral worries. As we stand at the edge of a future where innovation can reshape the human involvement with ways beforehand impossible, it is fundamental to consider the moral ramifications of our activities and the qualities that will direct us on this extraordinary excursion. The continuous mechanical development is a demonstration of human inventiveness and innovativeness, yet its definitive effect on society will be molded by our decisions today and the qualities that we maintain.

8.1 How advancements in technology continue to shape video app usage.

Headways in innovation have been instrumental in reshaping the scene of video application use. With each new advancement and leap forward, our utilization of video content has developed in huge ways. From the beginning of TV to the current period of web based stages, video application utilization is an impression of our evolving inclinations, ways of behaving, and the capacities of the innovation available to us.

The historical backdrop of video innovation utilization is an account of constant development. The TV, which upset the manner in which we consumed content, was one of the earliest instances of video innovation. It brought moving pictures and sounds into our homes, denoting a huge shift from radio and printed media. The presentation of variety TV, controllers, and satellite TV further extended the opportunities for video content utilization.

As innovation advanced, the appearance of videocassette recorders (VCRs) permitted us to record and playback video content whenever the timing is ideal. This noticeable a critical change in our relationship with video, empowering us to watch what we needed, when we needed. The appearance of VHS tapes and the resulting rivalry with Betamax prompted the foundation of an industry standard, molding the fate of home video utilization.

The ascent of DVDs got a jump video quality and stockpiling limit. The comfort of DVD menus, scene choice, and extra highlights improved the general survey insight. Be that as it may, the actual idea of DVDs additionally had constraints, including the gamble of harm and the requirement for extra room.

The genuine change of video application utilization started with the rise of advanced innovations and the web. Fast web associations made it conceivable to transfer video content, prompting the introduction of stages like YouTube, which permitted people to transfer and impart recordings to a worldwide crowd. This shift democratized content creation and utilization, as anybody with a web association could turn into a substance maker.

Headways in video pressure and real time innovations play had a crucial impact in the progress of online video stages. Designs like H.264 and the rise of versatile streaming have made it conceivable to convey great video content over the web, even on restricted transfer speed associations. These advancements have empowered the ascent of real time features, which have changed the manner in which we access and watch films and network shows.

The presentation of cell phones and versatile applications further sped up the change in video utilization propensities. Cell phones brought video content into our pockets, making it open anyplace and whenever. Online entertainment stages, as Facebook and Instagram, started to focus on video content, and brief video designs, like Plant and later TikTok, acquired notoriety. These stages saddled the abilities of cell phones, like cameras, touchscreens, and GPS, to make new types of video content and collaboration.

Live streaming turned into another peculiarity with stages like Periscope and later Facebook Live, which permitted clients to communicate real time video to their devotees. This ongoing cooperation opened up additional opportunities for content makers and crowds to participate in a more quick and individual manner.

As cell phones kept on advancing, the nature of inherent cameras and the handling force of these gadgets improved essentially. This prompted the ascent of portable video applications like Snapchat, which promoted the idea of "stories." Stories are short, fleeting video cuts that vanish after a set period. This arrangement fundamentally altered the manner in which we share minutes and encounters, stressing visual correspondence over text.

The ubiquity of stories and brief video cuts made ready for the hazardous development of TikTok, a stage that spins around short-structure, client created recordings set up with a good soundtrack. TikTok's calculation driven content revelation and proposal framework have made it a social peculiarity, impacting mainstream society, music, and dance patterns.

The development of video application utilization has not been restricted to diversion and online entertainment. The schooling area has likewise been significantly affected by headways in video innovation. The accessibility of great video content and live web based has changed the manner in which we learn. Stages like YouTube have become important assets for instructive substance, going from instructional exercises and talks to how-to guides and shows. Gigantic Open Internet based Courses (MOOCs) offer whole instructive projects web based, making learning available to a worldwide crowd.

The joining of video conferencing innovation into schooling has been additionally advanced by late worldwide occasions, like the Coronavirus pandemic. Virtual homerooms and internet learning have become fundamental instruments for teachers and understudies, taking into consideration far off cooperation and instruction on a remarkable scale.

In the corporate world, video conferencing stages like Zoom, Microsoft Groups, and Cisco Webex have become fundamental apparatuses for correspondence and coordinated effort. The capacity to hold virtual gatherings, online classes, and introductions has changed the manner in which organizations work. The innovation takes into consideration ongoing, up close and personal communications paying little heed to geological distance, lessening the requirement for movement and empowering remote work.

The headways in innovation have likewise altered the universe of diversion. The customary model of digital TV, with its proper timetables and restricted content choices, has confronted expanding rivalry from streaming stages. Administrations like Netflix, Amazon Prime Video, Disney+, and Hulu offer a huge library of on-request happy, including unique series and movies. These stages influence information investigation and personalization calculations to suggest content in light of client inclinations, upgrading the survey insight.

Because of the evolving scene, customary telecasters and media organizations have sent off their own web-based features. The "rope cutting" pattern, where watchers drop link memberships for real time features, has provoked the business to adjust to the computerized period.

Mechanical headways have additionally empowered the advancement of computer generated reality (VR) and expanded reality (AR) encounters. VR headsets and AR applications offer vivid and intelligent encounters that obscure the line between the physical and advanced universes. These advancements have applications in gaming, training, medical care, and different businesses, changing how we draw in with computerized content.

The gaming business has seen a critical development driven by progressions in innovation. Computer game control center, like the PlayStation, Xbox, and Nintendo Switch, have become all the more impressive and fit for delivering exceptionally practical illustrations and vivid interactivity. The ubiquity of online multiplayer games and eSports has made new types of social association and contest.

The approach of cloud gaming administrations, similar to research Stadia and NVIDIA GeForce Currently, can possibly disturb the gaming business further. These administrations permit clients to transfer games over the web, eliminating the requirement for strong neighborhood equipment and extending gaming availability.

Progressions in innovation have additionally formed the manner in which we access and consume news and data. Conventional print media has seen a decrease for computerized stages. News sites, web-based entertainment, and portable applications give ongoing updates and sight and sound substance. The utilization of video in news revealing and narrating has become progressively common, with live transmissions and on-the-ground detailing open to a worldwide crowd.

The coming of computerized reasoning and AI has changed video application use in various ways. Content proposal calculations investigate client conduct and inclinations to give customized video ideas. These calculations can keep clients drew in and work with content disclosure, however they have likewise confronted examination for possibly making "channel air pockets" and carefully protected areas.

Profound learning and PC vision innovations empower programmed content labeling and object acknowledgment, making it simpler to look for explicit video clasps and scenes. Programmed record and interpretation administrations improve availability and inclusivity in video content. Computer based intelligence driven video altering instruments, like programmed adjustment and variety remedy, engage content makers to create proficient quality recordings with insignificant exertion.

Regular language handling (NLP) and discourse acknowledgment have empowered voice-enacted video applications and menial helpers. These innovations permit clients to connect with video content through voice orders and perform errands like looking for recordings, controlling playback, and recovering data without manual info.

The advancement of deepfake innovation, which utilizes artificial intelligence to make hyper-reasonable controlled recordings, raises moral and security concerns. Deepfakes can be utilized for malignant purposes, for example, spreading disinformation and sabotaging trust in video content. This innovation additionally challenges the genuineness and validity of video proof, provoking the requirement for countermeasures and check apparatuses.

The reception of 5G innovation vows to additionally change video application use. 5G organizations offer altogether higher information paces and lower inactivity, empowering consistent web based of top notch video content on cell phones. This innovation will uphold expanded reality encounters, for example, AR gaming and vivid video, by giving the fundamental transfer speed and responsiveness.

The Web of Things (IoT) is another mechanical headway that influences video application use. IoT gadgets, outfitted with cameras and sensors, can transfer live video feeds and information to clients. This has applications in home security, savvy urban communities, and remote checking. The mix of video into the IoT environment improves situational mindfulness and information driven direction.

The development of video application use has additionally prompted worries about advanced protection and information security. The assortment of client information by video stages and the potential for information breaks have brought up issues about how individual data is dealt with and secured. Clients and controllers are progressively requesting straightforwardness and responsibility from innovation organizations in regards to information rehearses.

Content control and the battle against improper or destructive substance have become principal for video stages. Artificial intelligence driven content channels and human arbitrators are entrusted with observing and eliminating content that abuses local area rules. The harmony between free articulation and content balance stays a disagreeable issue, with continuous discussions about oversight, disdain discourse, and deception.

The progressions in innovation have disturbed customary plans of action and income streams for content makers and media organizations. While streaming stages offer new open doors for circulation, they have likewise achieved new difficulties as far as income sharing, copyright authorization, and the adaptation of content. Stages like YouTube and Jerk empower content makers to produce pay through promoting, sponsorships, and watcher gifts, making another class of advanced business people.

The multiplication of video application utilization has additionally impacted publicizing and advertising methodologies. Video advertisements and force to be reckoned with showcasing efforts have become unmistakable ways of drawing in crowds and advance items and administrations. The utilization of information investigation permits promoters to target explicit socioeconomics and measure the viability of their missions, expanding the profit from venture.

The union of innovation and video content has led to new organizations and patterns. Live web based, intelligent recordings, and 360-degree video encounters are reshaping the way in which we draw in with content. Computer generated reality is opening up new aspects for narrating and vivid encounters. These patterns challenge customary story structures and empower dynamic investment from watchers.

The improvement of cross-stage similarity and consistent combination across gadgets has made it workable for clients to begin watching a video on one gadget and progress forward another. The comfort of "observe anyplace" has turned into a central assumption for video application clients.

As innovation keeps on propelling, the fate of video application use holds significantly more groundbreaking prospects. The joining of video into daily existence, work, and instruction is probably going to turn out to be more consistent. Upgraded intuitiveness and personalization will offer clients a custom fitted and drawing in experience. The limits between the genuine and virtual universes will obscure further with the advancement of increased and augmented reality. Video content will assume a focal part in the manner we learn, work, convey, and engage ourselves.

Be that as it may, as video innovation keeps on advancing, moral, legitimate, and social difficulties will persevere. Issues of protection, information security, content control, and the mindful utilization of man-made intelligence driven advancements will require progressing consideration. Finding some kind of harmony between mechanical development and shielding individual privileges and cultural qualities will be a continuous test.

All in all, progressions in innovation have ceaselessly reshaped video application use, from the beginning of TV to the cutting edge time of streaming stages and cell phones. These developments have changed how we access, make, and associate with video content. The advancement of innovation, from fast web to computerized reasoning, has empowered customized encounters, continuous correspondence, and new arrangements. As 5G and IoT advancements keep on arising, the fate of video application utilization vows to be considerably more vivid and interconnected. Nonetheless, with these open doors come difficulties, including information protection, content control, and moral contemplations. The continuous change of video application use mirrors our persevering through longing for development and the flexibility of innovation to meet our advancing necessities and inclinations.

8.2 Emerging trends and future possibilities.

Arising patterns and future prospects are continually molding the world in which we live, from innovation and the economy to society and the climate. These patterns are not confined yet interconnected, affecting each other in complex ways. As we look forward to the future, it's fundamental to investigate these arising patterns and consider the potential outcomes they present for our aggregate future.

One of the most groundbreaking patterns is the proceeded with headway of innovation. This includes different parts of our lives, from the manners in which we impart and work to the strategies we use for transportation and amusement. The quick speed of mechanical advancement indicates that things are not pulling back.

Man-made reasoning (computer based intelligence) and AI are at the very front of this pattern. These advances have proactively started to influence different ventures, like medical care, money, and assembling. In medical care, computer based intelligence is assisting with early sickness conclusion and medication revelation, while in finance, it's utilized for algorithmic exchanging and risk appraisal. In the work environment, man-made intelligence driven robotization is smoothing out errands and changing the idea of work, starting discussions about the fate of occupations and the abilities expected to remain applicable in the gig market.

The Web of Things (IoT) is another innovation driven pattern. As additional gadgets and items become interconnected, we're seeing a huge change in how information is gathered, dissected, and used to work on our day to day routines. IoT applications range across different spaces, including savvy homes, shrewd urban communities, and modern cycles. The potential for further developed productivity, accommodation, and asset the executives is significant, however it likewise raises worries about information security and online protection.

Blockchain innovation, initially produced for cryptographic forms of money like Bitcoin, is currently being investigated for different applications past computerized monetary standards. Its true capacity in making secure and straightforward computerized records is being investigated

in regions, for example, store network the board, medical services records, and casting a ballot frameworks. Blockchain has the ability to upset the manner in which we store and trade worth and data, offering a decentralized and sealed framework.

Quantum processing is not too far off and could generally change the scene of computational power. While customary PCs use bits (0s and 1s), quantum PCs use qubits, which can address both 0 and 1 at the same time because of quantum trap. This considers quicker and more productive computations that could significantly affect cryptography, materials science, and medication revelation. Nonetheless, it likewise represents a critical test to existing encryption techniques and brings up issues about the security of computerized frameworks.

The digitalization of our day to day routines has critical ramifications for information protection. As more private data is gathered and dissected, inquiries regarding who possesses and controls that information become progressively significant. Information breaks and worries about the abuse of individual data have prompted conversations about information morals and guidelines. Finding some kind of harmony between the likely advantages of information driven experiences and individual security is a basic test.

The ascent of biotechnology is another remarkable pattern. Propels in genomics and quality altering strategies, like CRISPR, are opening up additional opportunities for customized medication, illness avoidance, and hereditary alteration. While these advancements hold extraordinary commitment, they likewise raise moral problems about the utilization of these innovations, including inquiries concerning hereditary protection, creator children, and unseen side-effects.

Environmentally friendly power and manageability are becoming focal issues notwithstanding environmental change and natural debasement. The progress to clean energy sources, for example, sunlight based and wind power, is speeding up. Energy capacity innovations, as cutting edge batteries, are essential for making environmentally friendly power sources more solid and available. Also, developments in transportation, for example, electric vehicles and hydrogen power modules, are having an impact on the manner in which we move individuals and products. The roundabout economy, which plans to limit squander and advance asset effectiveness, is getting some decent forward momentum as a practical way to deal with creation and utilization.

Worldwide wellbeing and general wellbeing have become the dominant focal point following the Coronavirus pandemic. The pandemic has uncovered the interconnectedness of our reality and the significance of worldwide collaboration in answering wellbeing emergencies. Telemedicine and telehealth have acquired noticeable quality as method for giving medical services while limiting actual contact. The turn of events and appropriation of immunizations have featured the difficulties and amazing open doors in biotechnology and global joint effort.

Segment patterns, including maturing populaces and urbanization, are reshaping social orders and economies. The maturing populace in numerous nations presents difficulties connected with medical care, social administrations, and annuities. Simultaneously, urbanization is prompting the development of super urban areas, significantly altering the manner in which individuals live and work. These patterns have huge ramifications for foundation, transportation, and lodging.

The eventual fate of work is going through a significant change. The ascent of remote work, advanced rapidly by the pandemic, is changing how and where individuals work. It has suggestions for office spaces, transportation, and metropolitan preparation. The gig economy and the idea of "adaptable work" are turning out to be more pervasive, testing customary business models and bringing up issues about employer stability and laborer assurances.

Manageability and ecological obligation are turning out to be progressively focal in strategic approaches. Organizations are embracing Corporate Social Obligation (CSR) and Natural, Social, and Administration (ESG) standards, with a developing accentuation on moral and economical practices. Shoppers are requesting more straightforwardness about the ecological and social effect of the items and administrations they use, and organizations are answering by embracing greener advancements and store network rehearses.

One more critical pattern is the improvement of brilliant urban communities. These urban communities are outfitting innovation to work on the personal satisfaction for their inhabitants. They use information investigation, sensors, and computerized foundation to upgrade transportation, diminish energy utilization, and work on open administrations. Savvy urban communities intend to make more proficient, economical, and reasonable metropolitan conditions. Be that as it may, this pattern additionally brings up issues about information security and the potential for observation.

The instructive scene is developing, with a developing accentuation on internet learning, distant training, and computerized assets. Gigantic Open Web-based Courses (MOOCs) offer adaptable, available learning valuable open doors, and colleges are progressively integrating on the web parts into their educational programs. The fate of schooling might see a mix of face to face and web based getting the hang of, empowering a more customized and open way to deal with information obtaining.

As society turns out to be more interconnected and dependent on computerized innovations, network safety has turned into a basic concern. Cyberattacks, information breaks, and data fighting posture huge dangers to people, associations, and state run administrations. The advancement of secure computerized frameworks and the insurance of basic foundation are first concerns to guarantee the wellbeing and uprightness of advanced networks.

Bioprinting, which utilizes 3D printing innovation to make living tissue and organs, can possibly change medical care. This innovation could address organ deficiencies and improve the opportunities for regenerative medication. In any case, it likewise brings up moral issues about the creation and utilization of living tissue and the potential for organ dealing.

Space investigation is encountering a resurgence, with both government space organizations and privately owned businesses assuming critical parts. The colonization of Mars, lunar missions, and space rock mining are only a couple of the potential outcomes not too far off. As space investigation propels, it can possibly reshape how we might interpret the universe, set out new financial open doors, and address asset shortage.

The idea of a "metaverse," an aggregate virtual shared space, is turning out to be progressively examined. This computerized domain could combine parts of online entertainment, computer generated reality, and increased reality, making another aspect for social connection, work, and amusement. The metaverse can possibly change the manner in which we associate, team up, and draw in with advanced content, yet it additionally brings up issues about security, personality, and the potential for habit.

The development of quantum processing is ready to alter computational power and critical thinking capacities. Quantum PCs can possibly handle complex issues, for example, mimicking quantum frameworks, upgrading supply chains, and breaking current encryption techniques. Quantum processing could reclassify what is computationally conceivable, prompting forward leaps in science, money, and innovation.

In the domain of energy, combination power holds guarantee as a clean, essentially boundless energy source. It duplicates the interaction that controls the sun by melding hydrogen particles into helium, creating huge measures of energy. Whenever tackled effectively, combination power could give a progressive answer for the world's energy needs and decrease dependence on petroleum derivatives. In any case, accomplishing controlled atomic combination has demonstrated to be a colossal logical and designing test.

Biodegradable materials and biomimicry are becoming integral to feasible plan and assembling. Researchers and designers are seeking nature for motivation in making materials and items that are both useful and harmless to the ecosystem. This pattern upholds the roundabout economy by diminishing waste and advancing mindful asset use.

The improvement of cutting edge materials, for example, graphene and carbon nanotubes, is empowering forward leaps in hardware, energy capacity, and aviation. These materials have one of a kind properties that make them unquestionably solid, lightweight, and conductive. As they become more reasonable and available, they can possibly change different businesses and lead to advancements in energy capacity and sustainable power.

The combination of man-made intelligence with remote helpers and chatbots is fundamentally impacting the manner in which we associate with innovation. Regular language handling (NLP) and discourse acknowledgment take into consideration more instinctive and human-like communications with machines. Simulated intelligence driven remote helpers, as Siri and Alexa, have become ordinary in our regular routines, from addressing inquiries to controlling brilliant home gadgets.

3D printing is growing past prototyping and into creation level assembling. This innovation is being utilized to make custom items, spare parts, and, surprisingly, whole structures. 3D printing is reforming supply chains by empowering on-request, confined creation and lessening the requirement for enormous inventories.

High level advanced mechanics and computerization are changing enterprises, from assembling to medical services. Cooperative robots, or cobots, are working close by people in plants, expanding efficiency and accuracy. In medical care, robots are helping with medical procedures and restoration, making operations more exact and less obtrusive.

Neurotechnology is at the cutting edge of understanding and upgrading the human mind. Cerebrum PC interfaces (BCIs) are permitting people to control gadgets and convey through their viewpoints.

This innovation can possibly change the existences of individuals with handicaps and open up new outskirts in human-PC collaboration.

The conceivable outcomes introduced by arising patterns are energizing and hold the possibility to shape the future in significant ways. Nonetheless, they likewise accompany difficulties and moral contemplations. As innovation keeps on propelling, inquiries regarding information protection, security, and the capable utilization of artificial intelligence and biotechnology become fundamental. Guaranteeing that these patterns are outfit to help mankind while moderating their dangers is a basic errand for legislatures, associations, and society overall.

All in all, arising patterns in innovation, biotechnology, maintainability, and numerous different fields are reshaping our reality in phenomenal ways. The conceivable outcomes introduced by these patterns are energizing and hold the possibility to address a portion of mankind's most squeezing difficulties. Nonetheless, they likewise accompany moral, social, and ecological contemplations that should be painstakingly figured out how to guarantee a prosperous and practical future. As we look forward, it's fundamental for screen these patterns, participate in discourse, and go with informed choices that shape our aggregate future to improve things.

Chapter 9

Society's Adaptation to Change

Society's capacity to adjust to change is an essential part of its flexibility and progress. Since the beginning of time, social orders have stood up to a huge number of changes, whether driven by mechanical progressions, ecological movements, social changes, or outside factors like pandemics or international occasions. Variation is a unique cycle that includes different parts of human existence, from the person to the group, and from the nearby to the worldwide level.

One of the most clear drivers of progress in contemporary society is innovation. The fast progression of innovation, especially in the domains of data innovation, man-made consciousness, and biotechnology, has changed the manner in which we live, work, and impart. This continuous mechanical upset has introduced a period of exceptional availability and data access. The boundless reception of cell phones, high velocity web, and computerized stages has meaningfully altered the manner in which we communicate with the world.

The versatility of society to these mechanical changes is apparent in different ways. Correspondence has become quicker and more open, associating people across huge distances progressively. Web-based entertainment has turned into a prevailing method of cooperation and data sharing, impacting everything from legislative issues to diversion. Internet shopping has upset customary retail, and remote work has re-imagined the idea of the work environment. These movements have changed the manner in which we live as well as set out new financial open doors and difficulties.

The ascent of man-made consciousness (computer based intelligence) is reshaping businesses, from medical care to fund. Computer based intelligence calculations are fit for handling huge measures of information, making expectations, and mechanizing assignments that were once viewed as past the capacities of machines. This can possibly further develop proficiency and exactness in different spaces, however it likewise brings up issues about the effect on business and the requirement for reskilling the labor force.

Biotechnology is one more outskirts of progress, offering prospects in customized medication, quality altering, and high level treatments. The versatility of society in this setting is apparent in the turn of events and use of quality altering strategies, like CRISPR, to address hereditary sicknesses. Biotechnology likewise holds possible in horticulture, empowering the improvement of dry spell safe harvests and decreasing the ecological effect of cultivating.

Society's transformation to mechanical change isn't without challenges. Issues connected with information security, network safety, and the dependable utilization of computer based intelligence are at the very front of public talk. The transformation cycle includes finding some kind of harmony between the advantages of innovation and the moral contemplations that emerge, including inquiries regarding information possession, observation, and the potential for algorithmic predisposition.

Environmental change is one more significant driver of progress in contemporary society. The rising recurrence and power of outrageous climate occasions, rising ocean levels, and changes in biological systems present huge difficulties. The flexibility of society despite environmental change includes both moderation endeavors to lessen ozone harming substance outflows and variation methodologies to adapt to the evolving climate.

Relief endeavors incorporate progressing to environmentally friendly power sources, diminishing fossil fuel byproducts from transportation and industry, and advancing maintainable land use. The versatility of society in this setting is obvious in the developing familiarity with ecological issues and the rising reception of environmentally friendly power advances. Supportability rehearses, like reusing, energy protection, and mindful utilization, are becoming standard, mirroring an aggregate obligation to tending to environmental change.

Transformation to environmental change incorporates measures like structure versatile framework, growing early admonition frameworks, and safeguarding normal biological systems. Beach front urban areas are putting resources into flood guards and metropolitan intending to get ready for rising ocean levels and outrageous climate occasions. Horticulture rehearses are developing to address changing weather conditions and guarantee food security.

The transformation cycle notwithstanding environmental change is likewise affected by social and conduct shifts. Reasonable ways of life, like decreasing meat utilization, utilizing public transportation, and preserving water, are turning out to be more far and wide. Developments like "Fridays for Future," started by youthful environment activists, are supporting for strategy changes and individual activities to address the environment emergency.

With regards to worldwide wellbeing, the Coronavirus pandemic has delineated society's versatility despite a significant general wellbeing emergency. The pandemic achieved abrupt and significant changes, influencing practically every part of life. It required quick reactions from legislatures, medical care frameworks, organizations, and people.

The flexibility of society in light of the pandemic is apparent in the fast turn of events and appropriation of immunizations. The worldwide academic local area teamed up to foster immunizations with extraordinary speed. The inoculation crusades showed the capacity of social orders to prepare and safeguard their populaces against a new and profoundly infectious infection.

The pandemic additionally sped up the reception of telehealth and telemedicine, empowering distant medical services access and diminishing the weight on medical care frameworks. Work environments progressed to remote and half breed models, changing the manner in which we work and impart. Web based business and food conveyance administrations experienced fast development, changing shopper propensities.

The pandemic highlighted the significance of general wellbeing measures, for example, veil wearing, social separating, and contact following. It additionally featured the requirement for readiness and the significance of logical aptitude in navigation.

Social variations were additionally clear during the pandemic. The significance of emotional well-being and prosperity earned respect, and people and networks tracked down inventive ways of remaining associated and support each other. Craftsmanship and diversion adjusted to a computerized world, with virtual shows, online theater, and streaming stages becoming essential wellsprings of social commitment.

Financial versatility was vital during the pandemic, as organizations and businesses needed to turn and conform to new circumstances. Eateries and retailers took on takeout and conveyance models, while the movement and accommodation enterprises executed severe wellbeing conventions. An organizations moved their creation to make fundamental clinical supplies, exhibiting flexibility in the midst of emergency.

The fate of work is an area of huge change and variation. The ascent of remote work, advanced by the pandemic, is changing customary office elements and setting out new open doors for adaptable business. The versatility of society in this setting incorporates the reexamining of office space plan, the advancement of computerized foundation, and the advancement of balance between fun and serious activities.

The gig economy is likewise changing the work market. Self employed entities and specialists are turning into a huge piece of the labor force, prompting conversations about work privileges, social security nets, and the eventual fate of business. The versatility of society includes resolving these issues and finding arrangements that balance the adaptability of gig work with specialist assurances.

As society adjusts to the changing idea of work, schooling is likewise advancing. Web based learning, Monstrous Open Web-based Courses (MOOCs), and distant training have acquired conspicuousness, offering more available and adaptable learning choices. The flexibility of society in schooling incorporates the advancement of computerized proficiency, the making of drawing in web based growth opportunities, and the reconsideration of customary instructive models.

The segment scene is one more area of massive change. Maturing populaces in numerous nations have suggestions for medical care, social administrations, and annuities. The versatility of society includes tending to the necessities of more seasoned grown-ups, advancing solid maturing, and reconsidering the idea of retirement.

Urbanization is changing social orders also, with the development of super urban communities and metropolitan regions. These progressions influence transportation, lodging, framework, and asset the board. The flexibility of society in this setting incorporates the improvement of maintainable metropolitan preparation, transportation arrangements, and lodging choices that address the issues of a quickly urbanizing world.

Ecological obligation and maintainability are vital to cultural flexibility. The progress to sustainable power sources, economical farming practices, and the advancement of the roundabout economy are instances of how society is tending to natural difficulties. The flexibility of society in such manner includes changing utilization designs, supporting eco-accommodating drives, and upholding for mindful natural arrangements.

One of the main social changes is the rising accentuation on supportability in strategic policies. Organizations are embracing Corporate Social Obligation (CSR) and Ecological, Social, and Administration

(ESG) standards. Customers are requesting more prominent straightforwardness and responsibility from organizations with respect to their natural and social effect. The flexibility

of society in this setting includes advancing moral and economical strategic approaches, diminishing ecological impressions, and guaranteeing capable production network the executives.

The improvement of shrewd urban areas addresses one more road of progress and versatility. These urban communities use information investigation, sensors, and advanced framework to upgrade transportation, decrease energy utilization, and work on open administrations. Savvy urban areas plan to make more productive, maintainable, and reasonable metropolitan conditions. The versatility of society in this setting includes embracing .

9.1 The societal and cultural implications of smartphone immersion.

The broad reception of cell phones significantly affects society and culture. As these strong gadgets have turned into an essential piece of our regular routines, they have achieved both positive and adverse results. This drenching in cell phone innovation has reshaped the manner in which we impart, work, collaborate with the world, and even characterize our personalities.

One of the main cultural ramifications of cell phone submersion is the change of correspondence. Cell phones have made it more straightforward than at any other time to interface with others, paying little mind to geological distance. Text informing, voice calls, and video talks are presently available readily available, empowering ongoing discussions with companions, family, and partners. This phenomenal degree of availability has reformed the manner in which we keep up with connections and has caused the world to feel more modest.

The ascent of online entertainment stages like Facebook, Instagram, and Twitter has additionally improved the social part of cell phone inundation. These stages give a space to individuals to share their lives, suppositions, and encounters with a wide crowd. The "like" culture and moment criticism components have affected the manner in which we develop our web-based personas and look for approval from our advanced companions.

In any case, this consistent availability has additionally raised worries about protection and the effect of web-based entertainment on emotional well-being. The capacity to record and divide each part of our lives has obscured the limits among the computerized and actual universes. The strain to organize an ideal web-based picture can prompt insecurities and uneasiness. Moreover, the assortment and business utilization of individual information by tech organizations have ignited banters about information security and the morals of advanced reconnaissance.

The working environment has seen huge changes because of cell phone drenching. Remote work, working from home, and adaptable work plans have become more normal, on account of the capacities of portable innovation. Representatives can remain associated, answer messages, and take part in virtual gatherings from practically anyplace. This flexibility has been particularly significant during the Coronavirus pandemic, as remote work turned into a need.

The versatility of society to remote work likewise features the significance of computerized framework and openness. Variations in web access and innovation assets have raised worries about inconsistent open doors for schooling and business. Spanning the advanced gap is fundamental for guaranteeing that the advantages of cell phone drenching are accessible to all citizenry.

Cell phones extraordinarily affect the manner in which we consume media and amusement. Web-based features, like Netflix, Hulu, and YouTube, have encountered outstanding development, making it simpler to get to a huge swath of content on our cell phones. These stages have moved the manner in which we stare at the Programs, films, and recordings, permitting us to pick what we need to watch and when we need to watch it.

The vivid idea of cell phone innovation has likewise prompted the ascent of portable gaming. Versatile games offer a helpful and compact type of diversion, and their ubiquity has extended the gaming crowd to incorporate individuals, everything being equal. The versatility of society to portable gaming is apparent in the different scope of games accessible, from easygoing riddles to complex multiplayer encounters.

While cell phones have brought accommodation and amusement into our lives, they have additionally raised worries about screen time and its effect on physical and emotional well-being. Unreasonable cell phone use can prompt issues like computerized eye strain and upset rest designs. The steady feeling given by online entertainment and gaming applications can add to compulsion like ways of behaving and adversely influence mental prosperity.

The versatility of society to cell phone innovation is likewise found in the manner we access data and remain informed. News applications and virtual entertainment stages have become essential wellsprings of data for some individuals. The constant idea of these stages permits us to remain refreshed on recent developments, however it additionally brings up issues about the spread of falsehood and the carefully protected area impact.

The instructive scene has been changed by cell phone innovation. Cell phones have become fundamental apparatuses for understudies and instructors the same. They empower admittance to internet learning assets, computerized course books, and instructive applications that work with customized opportunities for growth. The versatility of society to computerized training is clear in the rising notoriety of Huge Open Web-based Courses (MOOCs) and the fuse of innovation in customary study halls.

In any case, the digitalization of schooling additionally features the significance of tending to the computerized partition. Not all understudies have equivalent admittance to cell phones and the web, which can bring about variations in instructive results. The flexibility of society in this setting includes giving equivalent open doors to quality schooling and guaranteeing that innovation doesn't compound instructive imbalances.

The social ramifications of cell phone drenching stretch out to our imagination and self-articulation. The underlying cameras on cell phones have made photography and videography open to everybody. The simplicity of catching and altering pictures has prompted the democratization of visual narrating. Virtual entertainment stages have become grandstands for individual articulation through pictures and recordings, prompting the rise of powerhouses and content makers.

The flexibility of society to cell phone photography is obvious in the changing elements of photography as a fine art. Cell phone cameras have tested customary thoughts of photography, igniting banters about what is a "genuine" photo. The accommodation and availability of cell phone photography have democratized the medium, permitting more individuals to put themselves out there through visual narrating.

Cell phones have likewise reshaped the manner in which we consume music. Web-based features like Spotify and Apple Music have made it easy to get to a tremendous inventory of tunes and find new music. The versatility of society to this advanced music scene is apparent in the decay of actual music designs like Discs and the shift away from conventional radio for customized playlists and streaming suggestions.

The social ramifications of cell phone submersion are likewise reflected in the domain of writing and perusing. digital books and book recordings have become well known designs for consuming composed content, offering comfort and availability. The flexibility of society to computerized perusing is apparent in the ubiquity of tablets and perusing applications, which permit individuals to convey whole libraries in their pockets.

In any case, the digitalization of writing has likewise brought up issues about the eventual fate of actual books and the effect on customary book shops and libraries. The versatility of society in this setting includes finding some kind of harmony between advanced comfort and the protection of the social and verifiable meaning of printed books.

The gaming business has encountered a huge change due to cell phone submersion. Versatile gaming has turned into a huge market, with many games taking special care of different crowds. The versatility of society to portable gaming is apparent in the different gaming encounters accessible, from easygoing riddles to complex multiplayer games.

The social ramifications of cell phone gaming are likewise found in the manner we characterize gaming and the rise of esports as a standard type of diversion. The versatility of society to esports is obvious in the developing prominence of serious gaming occasions and the professionalization of esports as a lifelong way.

The joining of expanded reality (AR) and augmented reality (VR) into cell phone innovation has presented new components of social submersion. AR applications, as Pokémon GO, mix the virtual and actual universes, making intuitive and area based encounters. VR innovation, frequently matched with cell phones, offers vivid gaming and narrating encounters. The versatility of society to AR and VR is obvious in the energy and imaginative potential outcomes these advances offer, from craftsmanship establishments to virtual gallery visits.

The variation to AR and VR additionally brings up issues about the obscuring of the real world and virtual encounters. These advances challenge conventional ideas of the real world and virtuality, prompting conversations about the effect on personality, social associations, and the morals of vivid encounters.

The versatility of society to cell phone submersion likewise reaches out to the domain of wellbeing and prosperity. Wellbeing and wellness applications have acquired notoriety, empowering individuals to screen their actual work, nourishment, and emotional well-being. The versatility of society to these applications is clear in the developing interest in taking care of oneself and prosperity, as individuals look for ways of further developing their general wellbeing utilizing cell phone innovation.

9.2 How society is responding to these transformations.

The quick changes achieved by innovative progressions, changing work examples, and moving social standards have provoked different reactions from society. These reactions envelop both proactive transformations and the rise of new difficulties. As society wrestles with these changes, it's fundamental to inspect how people, networks, and organizations are answering these continuous changes.

One of the most prominent cultural reactions to these changes is the rising accentuation on computerized proficiency and instruction. As innovation turns out to be more coordinated into day to day existence, there is a developing acknowledgment of the significance of furnishing people with the abilities and information to explore the computerized scene. Schools and instructive establishments are integrating advanced proficiency into their educational programs, guaranteeing that understudies are customers of innovation as well as educated computerized residents.

Also, different associations and non-benefits are offering advanced proficiency programs for underserved networks to connect the computerized partition. These projects expect to give admittance to innovation, show advanced abilities, and engage people to partake in the computerized economy. This reaction mirrors a guarantee to making the advantages of innovative change open to all citizenry.

The changing idea of work, including the ascent of remote work and the gig economy, has provoked a reconsideration of work strategies and laborer privileges. Laborers' associations and work promotion bunches are upholding for fair wages, better working circumstances, and employer stability, even with regards to remote and gig work. The versatility of society in such manner includes rethinking work regulations to address the developing business scene and safeguard laborers' privileges.

Balance between serious and fun activities is one more part of the reaction to changing work designs. As people try to adjust their own and proficient lives in an undeniably computerized world, there is a developing interest for adaptable work game plans and strategies that focus on representative prosperity. Organizations are answering by offering adaptable timetables, remote work choices, and psychological well-being backing to oblige the changing necessities of their labor force.

The advancing job of innovation in medical care has brought about new methods of clinical benefit conveyance. Telemedicine and telehealth administrations have acquired noticeable quality, giving distant clinical discussions and administrations through computerized stages. This reaction to mechanical change improves medical services availability, especially for people in remote or underserved regions. It additionally offers helpful choices for routine clinical visits and conferences, diminishing the requirement for actual office visits.

Medical services foundations are likewise embracing electronic well-being records (EHRs) and computerized devices for diagnostics and therapy. The flexibility of society in this setting includes guaranteeing information security, protection, and adherence to medical services guidelines while outfitting the advantages of innovation for better understanding results.

The social reaction to cell phone inundation and computerized media utilization incorporates a reexamination of media proficiency and the effect of screen time. As people become progressively mindful of the expected results of over the top screen time, there is a developing development to advance careful media utilization and computerized detox. Media education programs intend to show people how to fundamentally examine the data they experience on the web, distinguish deception, and draw in with computerized media capably.

Moreover, there is a social shift towards focusing on eye to eye collaborations and human association in light of the predominance of computerized correspondence. Individuals are looking for ways of adjusting their on the web and disconnected lives, for example, assigning "without tech" hours, taking computerized holidays, and partaking in exercises that energize face to face socialization.

The reaction to advanced security and information security concerns includes upholding for more grounded guidelines and individual information insurance. Security promoters and policymakers are pushing for additional rigid information insurance regulations, like the European Association's Overall Information Assurance Guideline (GDPR) and the California Shopper Protection Act (CCPA). These guidelines expect associations to be more straightforward about their information assortment practices and give people more command over their own information.

Furthermore, people are turning out to be more proactive in defending their protection by changing their web-based entertainment settings, utilizing virtual confidential organizations (VPNs), and being mindful about the data they share on the web. Protection centered advances, similar to start to finish encoded informing applications, are additionally acquiring prevalence.

The cultural reaction to environmental change includes an aggregate obligation to manageability and ecological obligation. The progress to environmentally friendly power sources, for example, sunlight based and wind power, mirrors a worldwide work to lessen ozone harming substance outflows. Legislatures, organizations, and people are putting resources into sustainable power foundation and taking on eco-accommodating practices to alleviate the effect of environmental change.

The versatility of society is additionally found in the rising attention to preservation and asset the board. Endeavors to lessen squander, advance reusing, and execute roundabout economy standards mirror a guarantee to dependable asset use. Manageable agribusiness rehearses, for example, natural cultivating and accuracy horticulture, plan to diminish the ecological effect of food creation.

Urban areas are adjusting to environmental change by executing metropolitan arranging techniques that focus on maintainability, versatility, and low-carbon transportation choices. The advancement of green foundation, for example, metropolitan stops and green rooftops, mitigates the impacts of metropolitan intensity islands and decrease energy utilization. Furthermore, there is a developing development to make urban communities more walkable and bicycle cordial, empowering harmless to the ecosystem methods of transportation.

Worldwide wellbeing and general wellbeing have become focal worries because of pandemics and other wellbeing emergencies. The flexibility of society in this setting includes reinforcing medical care frameworks, putting resources into immunization improvement and conveyance, and upgrading global coordinated effort in light of wellbeing crises. The significance of logical mastery and information driven dynamic has been featured, underlining the job of science in protecting general wellbeing.

Segment changes, like maturing populaces and urbanization, are provoking transformations in different cultural areas. Medical care frameworks are adjusting to the necessities of a maturing populace by offering particular types of assistance for more established grown-ups and tending to progress in years related medical problems. Social administrations and annuity programs are advancing to help retired people and advance dynamic maturing.

Metropolitan regions are going through changes to oblige the development of super urban areas and urbanization. The versatility of society includes further developing transportation framework, tending to lodging reasonableness, and executing maintainable metropolitan arranging rehearses. Savvy urban communities are at the bleeding edge of this reaction, utilizing innovation and information investigation to upgrade the personal satisfaction for metropolitan inhabitants.

The reaction to the fate of work incorporates drives to set up the labor force for the changing business scene. Schooling and professional preparation programs are being upgraded to furnish people with the abilities required in a computerized and mechanized world. Long lasting learning and upskilling are becoming fundamental for remaining cutthroat in the gig market.

The gig economy is inciting conversations about work freedoms and the requirement for specialist insurances. Policymakers, work associations, and organizations are investigating ways of guaranteeing that gig laborers approach benefits, professional stability, and legitimate insurances. This reaction tries to find some kind of harmony between the adaptability of gig work and the prosperity of laborers.

Manageability and natural obligation are becoming focal in strategic approaches. Organizations are embracing Corporate Social Obligation (CSR) and Ecological, Social, and Administration (ESG) standards to adjust their tasks to moral and maintainable qualities. Purchasers are requesting additional straightforwardness and responsibility from organizations with respect to their ecological and social effect.

This social reaction mirrors a developing obligation to moral and maintainable practices, from diminishing carbon impressions and advancing dependable store network the executives to limiting waste and supporting eco-accommodating items and administrations.

The improvement of shrewd urban communities is a proactive reaction to the difficulties of urbanization and the requirement for more effective, supportable, and decent metropolitan conditions. Shrewd urban communities use information investigation, sensors, and advanced foundation to upgrade transportation, decrease energy utilization, and work on open administrations. The flexibility of society in this setting includes embracing the capability of innovation to further develop city life while resolving issues of information security and reconnaissance.